The muck f ...
giggles, supp
+ encouragemen
over the
years !

The Rebounding Revolution

❤ Theresa

⸎

A New Day, A New Way

The Rebounding Revolution

A New Day, A New Way

Theresa L. Bassett

ISBN: 0692667709
ISBN 13: 9780692667705

*In loving memory of my amazing grandmother, Mary,
and a boy who changed my life forever...Bailey...
May God forever keep you both as special angels right by His side.*

Acknowledgements

This book would never have been possible without the gift of so many individuals. Thank you, Kelley, for listening to me, truly hearing me, and loving me unconditionally. The blessing and timing of your love entering my life has been almost too profound to comprehend. God's perfect caretaking is so humbling to me! To my ultimate coach, the one who birthed me and literally life coached me along the way, every incredible baby step, my loving angel of a mother, Marilyn. Your grace and endless supportive vision for my highest and best has touched every word on these pages and has given me an amazing platform from which to voice my own vision into the world – thank you, Mom! A huge debt of gratitude to my children, Katrina, Arben, and Shelby, whose amazing journeys have only just begun and yet are already touching so many hearts with their unique selves…I love you beyond words! Thank you, Don and Sandy, Doug and Leah, for welcoming me into the Bassett clan at such a critical time in my path. The whole family has been wonderful to be a part of!

To one of my God-given creative muses, my father, for his continuous egging on and support to "keep on writing," keep on envisioning, and keep on creating. Thank you, Dad!

To my amazing sounding board of a brother, Scott – thank you, thank you, thank you for the endless conversations and willingness to help me cross any speed bump…for never losing faith in me. To all of my other loving extended family members especially Christine, Anne, Rob – your words, your thoughts, your prayers have helped me rise from the ashes a stronger, wiser version of myself. In fact, to all my aunts and uncles, who have all served as guides in faith, integrity, and wisdom in their own right. Throughout all my writing, I have also closely carried the hearts of all three of my special grandfathers – each of whom had a uniquely creative spirit that has served to inspire me. As inventors, entrepreneurs, and writers, their spirit lives on in me and puts wind beneath my wings daily.

To one of my dearest friends, Amy, for always loving me and being there. You have given me endless blessings – words can't even express. To Michele, who has literally given me the superfood for the journey – I wouldn't have been able to any of this without your contribution! To the entire team at Heart+Hammer who work daily to serve the world with their best, and who continue to bless me daily. This book began as one thing and continues to evolve all on its own – God is living and breathing through this work and for that I am profoundly grateful and humbled. And to all I haven't the space to mention and all that bless me with their energy in reading this work in years to come – thank you, thank you, thank you!

Yours in service,

Theresa

Foreword

When I first started writing Rebounding, it was 2009 and I merely started it as a journal exercise – as a way to clear my head and heal my heart. Well, actually, a way to stay sane in the midst of everything falling apart in my life. By the beginning of 2010, there was much news about the impacts from the financial fallout of the 2008 events in the U.S. – people having lost businesses, marriages, 401-k's. I sensed a deep need for a shared experience – that perhaps sharing what was going on with me would somehow offer comfort to someone else going through a setback. By April, 2010 I knew I had to repurpose my writing and create a book. That began a journey that I am still on today.

When I self-published the first edition of this book, I did not include my walk in faith or my relationship to Christ at all. I talk a little bit about that "coming full circle" and return to my Christian roots in the first chapter. I felt strongly that I was not to invest energy in marketing that book right after I completed it. I was a little disappointed in that – as a single mother experiencing the financial difficulties I had been, I was hoping to derive even a bit of income from the sales of that book. But God clearly instructed me to hold off and I took its listing off of Amazon.com as a result.

Nearly two years later, I finally got the green light to re-approach the project and was shown through prayer what I needed to do: rewrite the manuscript, include my relationship with God – in fact, put it at the center of not only my life but my book and my relationships, my business, my livelihood on every level – and republish. Now, many years later – nearly 7 years from its beginning, I offer you this enhanced second edition. The devotional section of this book was very powerful to write – I can only pray it will be equally powerful to pray on and read as an addition to my story.

I do not know what God has in store from here for this project – I only know I felt called to complete what I began. I have tried many times to even side burner or table this project, but I keep being brought back. As I watch world events unfold around me, I can only imagine what we will be rebounding from as individuals and as a collective. My prayer is that whomever, wherever, this book is meant to touch, it touches. My additional prayer is one of gratitude – God has revealed much to me throughout this project – much about my own humanness and much about His divine love and guidance and our need for obedience to the Holy Spirit's tugging at our heart and gut.   I feel so truly blessed to be even a very miniscule part of a bigger plan.

Introduction

"The Spirit of God *is* upon me; because
the Lord hath anointed me to preach
good tidings unto the meek; he
hath sent me to bind up the
brokenhearted, to proclaim liberty
to the captives, and the
opening of the prison to
them that are bound."

Isaiah 61:1

If you bought this book thinking that I was going to tell you about how beautifully I did a swan dive off the diving board of life and recovered after doing a giant belly smack, you have another thing coming. Rebounding is not always about perfectly moving through the stages of grief and turning right back around and carrying on or persevering despite the challenges. Rebounding is about the art of rediscovering and recreating yourself after experiencing personal and professional setbacks, about granting yourself grace and radical forgiveness in the midst of chaos. It is about RECEIVING grace and radical forgiveness from our Lord and savior, Jesus Christ, and KNOWING you don't have to do it all alone.

These setbacks may come in the form of major financial losses such as a bankruptcy or foreclosure. They might come in the form of a failed business, divorce, or health crisis. For everyone they are something a little bit different and yet in the range of experiences…in the emotional phenomenon accompanying these challenges in their aftermath, we can find common ground. No matter what your education or background, your beliefs or the situation, when you run into one of these challenges, and trust me, you WILL…you will be called to respond in some way.

It is this response that I am writing about here. In the attempt to tell you about my struggle to rebound after my own personal and professional failures, I will also attempt to cope with and help you cope with the very setbacks that are in front of both of us…you and me, together. Upon this very writing, I am rebounding from one of the lowest spots in my own personal and professional life and yet God has graced me the energy and perspective to persevere. I am not writing from a "been there, done that" perspective but rather from one of a "done that many times, and am still doing that" perspective. I emphasize the PROCESS, not the OUTCOME, throughout this book, because in my own experience much too much emphasis is put on getting there rather than the process that we undertake to keep moving on the path. And yet it is in actually embracing the journey that we discover true freedom and the grace to BE. To be imperfectly, uncontrollably, unstoppably ourselves…always a work in progress.

The economic, social, and familial realities of the world outside our doors are not currently creating an easy pill to swallow. We turn on the news and all we hear is strife and turmoil. We turn off the news and we face the stress and turmoil in our own living rooms. My hope is that perhaps in sharing my own story, you will find comfort and strength and a sense of not being such a lone wolf after all. Yes, it happens to other people in a very real way and you too can recover. I, after all, am rebounding and moving forward by coming out and talking to you. And that is enough for me today.

I'm Theresa Bassett and I'm very grateful to be here – thank you, thank you, thank you for letting me be a part of your journey today.

I believe without a shadow of a doubt that everything that has happened in my life, everything in my life has led me perfectly right here.

I also believe without a shadow of a doubt that everything that has happened in your life, everything in your life has led you perfectly here. God brought us together here to help one another. What we do with that opportunity from here is up to us.

I am here to help you see something you need to see, feel something you need to feel, or learn something you need to learn and you are here to help me see something I need to see, feel something I need to feel, or learn something I need to learn. In knowing that, I am totally humbled and blessed beyond measure to be here today with you.

We have a loving God to thank for that and for that let us give him all the glory.

From a very young age, I was made aware, as Dr. Wayne Dyer is known to have said, I was not a human being having a spiritual experience but in fact a spiritual being having a human experience. The Holy Spirit breathed this KNOWINGNESS into me at the age of 8 years old and I was acutely aware that I was not in control. That my job was to pray, to listen, to act. It was the first lesson I remember journaling – in fact, I still have the journal.

And yet, even knowing that, I lost my way somewhere along the path and had to find my way back.

I grew up Catholic. I was a regular church goer...in fact, I almost became a nun. After traveling to Rome, I heard my calling to be a mother instead and felt I no longer needed to be served by a religious institution. I left the church.

I have been a student of the personal growth, leadership, and human development industry since I was 13 years old. I have read thousands of pages, spent thousands of hours on personal growth. I have always loved it – the writing of the sages, the men and women who were inspired to record their words of wisdom. I eat, sleep, and breathe the stuff and have for over 30 years. They say that reading 780 books is roughly the equivalent of a PhD's worth of information –if that is the case, I am several PhD's into this amazing genre. It is my passion – I couldn't even buy enough books

– in fact, I now have formed a non-profit called Bailey's Books that donates self-help, inspirational and motivational literature to places people may most need it – food kitchens, shelters, agencies that serve the poor or disadvantaged. Those books saved my life. I should say, the Lord inspiring me to read all those books saved my life – several times over in fact.

I have walked across the coals with Tony Robbins, I've been personally trained by Stephen Covey in Park City Utah for a week, soaking up his wisdom. I have pilgrimaged to Rome, consulted bishops, I have confessed at the knees of a Cardinal, I have lived in Europe and dated counts and the body guards of princes. In Switzerland, after leaving the church, I married my first husband, a non-practicing Muslim Albanian from Kosova. I supported a third world village for over a decade. I saved refugees in Macedonia from an uncertain fate by helping them get transferred to the U.S., getting several area churches to sponsor them. I successfully ran two marathons, even after ending up on crutches after Marathon #1. I have personally sold over $250 million dollars worth of real estate, goods, or services. I have contributed to the building of three million-dollar businesses. I have helped over 200 business owners create major breakthroughs in their success or productivity.

I don't tell you these things to impress you but to impress upon you that you are never done learning. You are never done being torn down only to be built up.

In 2001, 6 ½ months pregnant, my husband abandoned me emotionally, physically, and financially I was left unprepared, a poor grad student with a 13-month old daughter and a baby boy on the way. I was unable to keep my home because I couldn't make the payments – I moved back in with my parents and I asked them to give me 3 months there in order to have the baby and move into an apartment. They were generous and loving always and still are to this day. They would've have given me 3 years if I needed it but I asked for 3 months.

I went on welfare, food stamps and child care assistance. I got Bell's Palsy, half my face became paralyzed, and I was in a car accident one day on the way home from the state welfare office, where I had just gotten turned down for an emergency grant that would allow me to pay the deposit on my apartment's electric account. I made $850/month as a grad assistant at the time and I cleaned houses and taught community college classes in between nursing my newborn to try and make ends meet. I remember sitting on the curb looking at my smashed in car, my daughter crying while I held the hand of one and had the other attached to my chest for comfort. My mom came to pick me up while the tow truck came to get my car. I had scraped together $2200 from side jobs to buy that now smashed Volvo. Life was not giving me any breaks.

I persevered. I kept teaching and I finished the courses in my degree program. I nursed my son to 15 months. Largely because it cut down on my baby food needs and gave me a way to keep him quiet while I studied into the nights.

I came home one day and my electric was turned off, it was winter. Something snapped in me and I knew I had to do something different. I drove to the corner car dealership and applied for a job in sales. I sold Chevy's, I became the number one salesperson in the dealership – and to this day, the #1 woman since the dealership opened in 1967. I learned something important there – I could sell. I mean really sell. It changed my life. I got my first $10k monthly check 4 months into it. I hadn't even made $10k in the previous year all together!

I went back to real estate and new construction where I had gotten my career start before having kids. I sold homes the way I sold cars. Like I needed to sell 20 a month to make my goals. Lol…my boss actually called me up one day and said "Theresa, seriously, you don't have to sell as many houses as you did cars!"

I pulled myself and my children out of poverty and dropped the welfare. I went on to become the first million-aire in my family 36 months later. I held 12 residential prop-erties as investments at one point, was debt-free, living on 20% of my income, and was astonished at what I was able to accomplish.

In 2006, I stretched my entrepreneurial wings and opened my first business, a boutique coaching agency called Inspire. I was on fire to take all my personal coaching, train-ing, sales and marketing experience and change people's lives and businesses. We had over $400k in sales in Year 1 and then I landed my biggest deal yet, a $2.5M gig for a local HR firm, building them a training institute with a coach-ing component. A $30,000+ plus retainer per month plus profit-sharing at 50%. The checks started coming ….only 12 months earlier I had put a sticky note on my computer that my goal was to make $30k a month.

Again, I was astonished at what I could accomplish when I put my mind to it. I was happily remarried by the time, had a beautiful $400k home that I had purchased myself prior to getting married, was traveling regularly, was speaking to groups regularly and coaching. I was living my dream. I thought I had made it to the peak of the mountain.

The problem was, I was missing a critical element, I was forgetting the very first lesson I had learned, getting caught up in my own ability.

In 2008, the house of cards fell down. All the way down. My rags to riches story was not over. Not even close.

The HR company that hired mine, as it turns out, was shut down by the IRS for payroll tax fraud....

To make a long story short, I lost everything I had worked so hard to achieve. Everything right down to the marriage and the money and the house. All my properties, everything. I had invested in something and lost it all. I felt betrayed... Betrayed once again in my marriage (I mean I really thought this time was forever truly), betrayed by these business owners who had lured me and my baby company into their fraudulent mess, betrayed even by God.

And then, I was betrayed by my own body. My metabolism shut down and I gained 60 pounds, my adrenals were kaput, my body could process no more stress. I gained weight, I got shingles, and I developed fibromyalgia. I was so broken and inflamed, it hurt to be outside in the wind at one point – the slightest touch hurt my skin. I was bankrupt, alone again, and sick.

Talk about a lesson in humility. Rags to riches and back to rags again. They say that God doesn't call the qualified but instead qualifies the called. To this day, I believe strongly that this trip to my own personal wilderness was, in fact, part of my qualification process.

Welfare, living with friends…even at one point, living out of my car….weeks of not knowing where food and gas money was coming from. I got jobs, I tried to go back to real estate as my fall back - but I had lost my mojo, I felt lost, despondent, insecure in my abilities and I doubted my own judgment. I had also found my calling in being an entrepreneur and I found it very very difficult to go back to being an employee. I did the best I could, day by day. I persevered. I discovered a premium nutrition program that healed my body.

But I was by that point, depressed. Psychologically unemployable, I felt like everything I tried to do failed to move me forward. I even started a journal, turned it into a book called *Rebounding: Getting Up and Getting Over It* and tried to turn my lemons into lemonade. I even self-published that book with the hopes of marketing it, beginning some speaking events again. Reenergizing and restarting my business.   It is just so hard to start again when your belief in yourself has been so sorely challenged. And I hit some HUGE resistance in my prayers when I started to pray about marketing the book. I was literally told to STOP and not proceed in marketing the book. I was so upset – I had thought that was a financial ticket out of the hell of poverty that I was living in yet again. Literally every piece of clothing I owned came from Goodwill, at one point I was without a car for almost a year – I scraped change together to buy enough decent clothes at Goodwill to begin selling real estate again. I was so very lost.

I had begun to pray again regularly. I had been praying daily leading up to the opening of my business in 2006, had even received the image for my logo in a prayer session, felt that everything I did as a part of that coaching and training business was divinely inspired. And wasn't my quick success proof that my discipleship was being rewarded?

What I failed to see until years later, was that I had left God out of my business once I opened the doors, I had left him out of my book entirely and out of my recovery attempts really. He began to show me that I needed to come full circle – I needed to come back into the church, back into community, into a renewed relationship with him. It wasn't enough to try and pull myself up by my own bootstraps this time – I NEEDED MORE.

I was led back into a non-denominational Christian church and rebaptized in 2012. I began to talk to Jesus Christ again. While in my first marriage, I had begun apologizing and hiding my relationship with Christ. I focused my prayers on God, a more universal God and did so also in my coaching business. I considered myself Christian but was unchurched from the age of 23 to 41.

God revealed to me through prayer that I needed to rewrite the book and stop disregarding my relationship with

Christ and its role in my journey. I persevered and began rewriting the book in 2012…I finished it one week ago today. In the meantime, I have found the love of my life, my best friend, and am married to him, celebrating our first anniversary next week. We successfully run and manage a full circle marketing and advertising agency that specializes in breathing new life into businesses and brands. We build our business on the Golden Rule and we pray over every decision before we make it…together.

I now understand that I am responsible for sharing my story with you. See, the revolution we are starting is a Rebounding Revolution. It is about discovering a new way, experiencing a new way of doing business, of recovering, of living life. Not only letting God in but truly letting him sit in the driver's seat. Co-creating WITH Him and giving him all the glory for the ability, not creating and pushing and striving on my own and then praying for delivery from my own messes. For it only through embracing our perfect imperfection and the grace that is available through his unconditional love that we are truly ever free. It is also about understanding we are not in it alone, we are not designed to do it alone. This book uses numerous references to Scripture, appropriately, but also includes secular quotes, recognizing that God's wisdom first and foremost is given to us through His Word contained in the Bible.

The other major thing that this book hopes to accomplish is to emphasize that no matter what we are facing, there are always blessings to be found in the rubble. They may come sneakingly disguised as hardships, but even as such, those hardships are the very things that build capacity, compassion, and core strength in us. They are also the challenges we need to open up to turning to a source bigger than ourselves – truly open ourselves up to letting go and letting God.

Why is it that only once we are forced onto our knees that we ever truly look up?

I believe without a shadow of a doubt that everything that has happened in my life, everything <u>in</u> my life has led me perfectly right here.

I also believe without a shadow of a doubt that everything that has happened in your life, everything <u>in</u> your life has led you perfectly here.

We were brought here perfectly together...to help each other in some way. I am here to help you see something you need to see, feel something you need to feel, or learn something you need to learn and you are here to help me see something I need to see, feel something I need to feel, or learn something I need to learn. In knowing that, I am totally humbled and blessed beyond measure to be here today with you.

See, I planned originally to be a success author and motivational coach – I didn't plan to "specialize" in falling down!

Well, I may be an expert at falling down but I am an absolute amazing authority on getting back up because of my relationship with our loving, loving God.

God Bless you.
Thank you, thank you, thank you.

Table of Contents

Acknowledgements · vii
Foreword ·ix
Introduction ·xi

PAST

I.   Wounded · 3
II.   Facing the Truth · 9
III. Living in the Past vs. Living in the Light · · · · · · · · 14

PRESENT

IV.   How Do You Move Forward? · · · · · · · · · · · · · · · · · 25
V.   You are Worth the Best of Care · · · · · · · · · · · · · · 41
VI.   Grieving our Losses · 49
VII. Up and Down Cycles: Working Together for Good · · 58

The 30-Day Rebounding Revolution Devotional

FUTURE

VIII. Envisioning a Better Way…or a Better Day · · · · · 147
IX.   Rising Up to Overcome · 153

About the Author · 159
Select Bibliography · 163
Special Opportunities and Offers · · · · · · · · · · · · · · 165

"If you are swept off your feet, it's
time to get on your knees."

– FRED BECK

Past

I.

Wounded

rebound:

noun 1: a movement back from an impact

2: a reaction to a crisis or setback or frustration

verb 1: spring back; spring away from an impact
- Merriam-Webster Dictionary

When I started out, I walked on air. I had the brains in my head and the shoes on my feet, as Dr. Seuss so aptly wrote, and I really could not be beat. I confidently plunged myself, my family, and my finances in to my new business venture. I was going to beat the odds by being diligent and smart, by tracking down whatever resources I needed to carry on. I was going to offer value and insight...we were going to change the world. I started a coaching and training agency that was equipped with the most positive people in the world – surely we could beat the odds if anyone could! I was in the self-development industry – I taught people how to be strong, to persevere by digging deep…surely nothing could drag me down.

A little under two years later, we had lost our largest client due to fraud and bankruptcy issues, and had no other major sources of revenue to carry the company. Having invested my life's savings, leveraged all my sources of credit and some of my husband's, I was maxxed out. I liquidated all the assets of the company that I could, including the office building itself, paid off what I could and with my tail between my legs, found myself sitting on over $140,000 of personally-secured debt. I hadn't been smart enough to put all the debts of the company in the company name and so I couldn't file for corporate bankruptcy and I was literally left stuck, holding the bag. Sure there were other people I could blame but I was to blame too. No matter how I sliced and diced it, I looked into the future and it looked grim. Little did I know that the fallout of this one event would have me sliding down a slippery slope into a kind of depression and a seemingly never-ending stream of financial challenges for years and years to come before any kind of rebound was in sight.

On top of it, the economy and my fall-back industry, real estate, was taking a major beating. I had nowhere significant to turn. After these years of self-employment, with two small children needing to be picked up from school, etc. I was hesitant to take a "job." I did for awhile, thinking that getting some steady income would help us get back on our feet, but the company turned out to not be so stable itself and I left it several months later (good thing as the company closed its doors a few weeks after I left). Unemployed, without any company left to speak of, holding all this life experience, baggage, and debt, I was floundering in a soup made up of confusion, despair, anger, fear, and borderline depression. It had been almost a year since things had hit the fan, and yet I still wasn't breathing a normal rhythm yet. I plunged myself into an intense exercise routine, thinking that was a good way to work off stress and lose unwanted pounds; although it did manage to keep me sane, I couldn't lose weight due to the internal stresses, and after awhile it felt less than productive. I sent out rounds and rounds of resumes – I wasn't qualified for many jobs outside of my industry and the job market was flooded with people like me due to unemployment being at record levels. I received a few phone calls and got a couple of interviews – mostly entry level sales jobs in industries that I had no interest.

I think the thing that made it harder than anything was that my business had been about coaching and training – empowering people to be their best. At MY best, I knew that I loved to speak, train, consult, and write. I just couldn't seem to get that to pay. Spiritually, I felt wounded in a very deep way. Here I had given my all, everything I knew how to give, to this business and the bottom line was, my best wasn't good enough. How was I going to get up the courage to try anything that really put me out there again, when I may have to face the same failure? My body's stress response system was shot – I wasn't sure if I even had the internal resources to pull it off and yet a job wasn't materializing nor did it seem like that was the long term answer. I was caught between my negative emotional space and the hard realities of the world.

And yet the economy was not going to support my wallowing and processing for long. My husband's work was also being threatened by the economic downturn in the building industry and we had too much personal overhead, having bought a larger, more expensive home while we were making plenty of money. That had upgraded our lifestyle and our budget. There were so many places we needed to make corrections and yet I felt like a deer in the headlights – how was I going to get myself out of this funk and productively tackle the challenges of the hour?

On the surface I was fighting the good fight – I had some part-time things lined up that were keeping me busy here and there. I was grocery shopping, preparing holiday meals, entertaining, helping kids with homework. I even bought a new puppy and began training her. I was still exercising, I had been to a therapist, was still talking to my coach regularly...all the things I was supposed to be doing. On the surface. Beneath that, however, was an inability to handle the hard stuff. I had a pile of bills and paperwork that was neglected on my desk (that I now avoided like the plague), I was blowing off prospective and current clients, I was haphazardly handling appointments, I was lying about feeling okay, doing okay, and being okay. I was not okay. Yes, in moments here and there I was, but not really.

I asked my then-husband, Rob, how he had felt, how he handled the bankruptcy of a company he had once had. He said he was the bread-winner and he didn't have much time to think about it – he just had to get on with it. His response added a second layer of guilt to the equation – the guilt of not being able for whatever reason to "just get on with it." I had tried to get a job and seemed to fail – I had tried to restart my company, even got a few clients, but was failing to keep them because I just didn't have the internal energy to carry it. I was stuck in a pit and needed out.

Now I wish I could say that hindsight was 20/20. That I could look back and figure out what exactly went wrong so that I could move forward, learn from it, and never regret again. I had bits and pieces of it – but I couldn't figure out why, in pursuing the thing that I felt called to do, I had experienced this level of failure. The one thing that I kept coming back to was my coaching training and feeling sure that my intuition had been right on. I <u>was</u> called to be a writer, speaker, coach, and consultant. I <u>was</u> called to be a business owner. I <u>was</u> called to be independent. Those things I knew – I just had to figure out how to make a living doing it.

I also had to get beyond feeling like a personal failure just because my business failed. What is that expression? "Don't take it personally"?? Hard not to when it is your butt on the line and your bill collectors are calling daily. Hard not to when every day you have reminders of all that you aren't doing, all that you weren't good enough to be. So let's see, I'm supposed to not take it personally and yet take 100% responsibility and accountability for myself. Yes, that's it – that solves everything! Not.

> *The two hardest things to handle in*
> *life are failure and success.*

Failed in business	Age 22
Ran for legislature	Age 23
Again failed in business	Age 24
Elected to legislature	Age 25
Sweetheart died	Age 26
Had a nervous breakdown	Age 27
Defeated for Speaker	Age 29
Defeated for Elector	Age 31
Elected to Congress	Age 37
Defeated for Congress	Age 39
Defeated for Senate	Age 46
Defeated for Vice President	Age 47
Defeated for Senate	Age 49
Elected President of the United States	Age 51

The record of Abraham Lincoln.

> What age would you have given
> up? Or have you already?

II.

Facing the Truth

Michelango's huge statue of David was produced from a single block of granite weighing several tons. The block of granite was rejected a century before the master sculptor used it as being unfit for a work of sculpture, yet out of this reject he fashioned his beautiful and inspiring masterpiece. Failure need never be final when faith is present.

– ROY L. LAURIN

There comes a point when the reality of the situation you are in really sinks in – it IS what is real. The gravity of the task at hand, unraveling the mess, recovering, persevering and moving on can seem overwhelming. "How did I get here?" is the natural question that arises. The trouble with that question is that it leaves you going down the road of the past again... and again...and again. While some questioning is healthy – this is how we will learn and hopefully not repeat the same life lessons – too much of a good thing is no longer good.

Ruminating over how you got here is not going to help you move forward. At some point reality will have to sink in.

I have a tendency to live in a remarkably optimistic world – the grass really is greener in my world most of the time. There is always a silver lining. Sometimes to get to the point that reality sinks in, it takes being backed into the "must" corner. I call it this because it is the point where you have reached no reasonably good alternative. You can no longer avoid, run from, hide in your despair, paint a rosy picture, justify it away, or take a vacation from the truth. Something happens to make this corner appear. The bank puts the fore-closure notice on your door, the electricity goes out, your spouse packs up and leaves, you get sick, or something equal-ly jarring that stops you momentarily in your tracks. The truth of the situation is now in your face and you, my friend, are now in the "must" corner.

You <u>must</u> face reality.

Personally I have been pushed into this corner three times that I can remember vividly. You do, by the way, tend to remem-ber these moments vividly because they are life changing, char-acter-shaping moments. Your back is against the wall and you have to choose. Are you going to choose to rise above, handle it; or are you going to let it break you?

The first time I visited this corner, it was at the end of my first marriage. It was a bright sunny day and we were in a local park to talk at my husband's request. Really we were there because he had to tell me that he wanted our so-called "temporary" separation to be permanent. I remember looking up at the blue blue sky in disbelief that this was actually happening to me – that I was really HERE. I was not being given the option of working it through any longer, we were at the crossroads and I had to choose my response. In those moments, I don't know if you are actually really conscious of the choice in front of you but in my memory I was. After getting over the disbelief and letting the grieving of the moment settle into my aching heart, still looking at that blue sky, I felt gratitude for being me, still being whole, and being able to rise above even this hurt.

It wasn't the optimist speaking then – there was no such "oh, everything is going to be alright" nonchalantly being thrown out there. No, this was more of a grounded, deep sense of KNOWING that I could be okay, that I was going to choose life and love over death and giving up. I was, after all, in the "must corner," I had a beautiful toddler daughter and a son on the way. I had no money, no home, no job, and no marriage but I had my health, my loving family, my babies, and my inner strength; my indomitable spirit. And of course, I had God right there all along.

Why is it so often that as humans we have to wait to get pushed into that unfortunate corner before we realize what we have and where we really are in life? I have asked myself this question so many times…why must we wait until it is imperative to know what we are truly made of? I can actually relate to what extreme sports fanatics are after – the adrenaline rush of feeling the core of yourself rise to the real challenge of living and….well, LIVE.

No one can take those moments from you and fortunately or unfortunately, we can't manufacture them either. Something probably happened in your life to push you into that corner or you wouldn't be reading this book. I am sorry you had to get there but at some point you have to give absolute thanks for those defining moments. You are seeking wholeness again, healing, and you are desiring the ability to move past it. See, it hasn't broken you after all, has it?

Hopefully, you are picking up on something by now that resonates with what you have been through. I am hoping that you will see how remarkable and adaptable you are. How resilient and capable. How you can choose gratitude and love even in the darkest moments. I have complete faith that once backed into the "must" corner, you will emerge triumphant and stronger than ever before, if that is what you choose. God has you in the palm of His mighty hand. Even if up until now you did not acknowledge it.

When the great Polish pianist, Ignace Paderwski, first chose to study the piano, his music teacher told him his hands were much too small to master the keyboard.

When the great Italian tenor, Enrico Caruso, first applied for instruction, the teacher told him his voice sounded like the wind whistling through the window.

When the great statesman of Victorian England, Benjamin Disraeli, attempted to speak in Parliament

*for the first time, members hissed him into silence
and laughed when he said, "Though I sit now,
the time will come when you will hear of me."*

Henry Ford forgot to put reverse on his first car.

*Thomas Edison spent two million dollars on an
invention which proved to be of little value.*

*Albert Einstein failed his university
entrance exams on his first attempt.*

Don't give up because you failed the first time.

*The only time you must not fail
is the last time you try.*

— CHARLES F. KETTERING

When was the last time you tried your
best without fear of failure?

III.

Living in the Past vs. Living in the Light

> *"I have been driven many times to my
> knees by the overwhelming conviction
> that I had nowhere else to go. My
> own wisdom and that of all about me
> seemed insufficient for the day."*

— ABRAHAM LINCOLN

Cutting to the chase, the ability to live in a space of owning our unique power and feeling gratitude for all, recognizing that **all of it** is a gift from God - is our end goal here. The fact of the matter is, no matter what form your particular set back came in, you have something remarkable to be grateful for. Maybe the loss was just what you needed to jar you out of the unconscious habits of living your daily life and make you face the incredible host of choices you have in front of you every day. The choice to be happy or not. The choice to love or not. The choice to take care of yourself or not. The choice to move on or not. Those choices existed even before you had this experience. They have existed from the moment of your birth because God gave us free will. What an amazing gift and responsibility. Our level of "response – ability" is directly impacted by how conscious we are of these choices in and around us all of the time. Our gratitude, our choice to live in good stewardship for our blessings, our attitude directly impacts our experience each and every moment.

Our ability to adapt and change and make positive choices, leading to momentum, is the difference between success and failure. It isn't determined by anything *external*, it is entirely determined by how we choose *internally*. I see an incredible waste of energy and wisdom every day. Potential being spent on living in the past…living in the past in a state of inaction, fearing mistakes, not trusting our own judgment, or simply not knowing how to get away from the hurt. Nothing keeps us stuck better than inaction. It perpetuates fear and regret.

That being said, we all have unique things that motivate us and keep us away from that place of inaction and fear and doubt. For me, there is nothing more powerful than taking in powerful words of positivity and inspiration. I wouldn't care if it was written on the back of a cereal box or in toothpaste on my bathroom mirror – positive words help me create positive thoughts and that makes all the difference! I've realized that when I may have gotten stuck in my own negative self-talk traps, it is because I got away from reading or listening to things that motivate and inspire me. I got further away from God and His Truth. I got lazy and fell into the radio and TV traps and only took in words from sources that didn't have motivation or inspiration on the top of their list of desired outcomes. Many times we take in the negative thoughts, words, or feelings of others on a consistent, daily basis without even realizing that we are doing it. It is almost impossible to participate in media of any kind and not meet a negative image or idea or report. The world is fascinated with sensationalism and we have to decide ahead of time how we wish to handle that. We can also get stuck listening to other people's story of negativity, drama, and victimization under the guise of "sympathy" or "empathy" and not realize how deeply it is effecting the messages that are informing our own thoughts and feelings. Garbage in, garbage out!

There are three categories of inspiration that I recommend you participate in regularly to set up a sort of inner defense shield against inaction. They appeal to the senses and do wonders to feed the soul and keep us motivated. They are: artistic, natural, and verbal.

Artistic

Artistic inspiration can come from anything that you create or anything that someone else created. Music, poetry, visual arts such as paintings, photography, and dance are all forms of art that are important to enjoy on a regular basis. They tend to elevate and broaden our perspectives, make us feel expansive, keep us in touch in a unique way with our innate gifts, and enhance the gratitude that we can feel about living. We can never anticipate the effect that exposure to art will have on us, and yet it is very rare that we aren't touched in some way when we consciously reach out for it.

For those that don't consider themselves creative, I strongly encourage you to try it in any form that seems approachable – even if that means grabbing your children's crayons and scribbling on a piece of paper now and then! We were all born with creative abilities and it is part of our nature to want to express that in some way. We have buried those impulses and intuitions many times beneath many layers, including those of responsibility and "maturity." We all remember feeling creative as children. We had imaginations then, didn't we?! If you haven't used your imagination or creative side in awhile, that doesn't mean it isn't there waiting to get out! We can gain remarkable insights and experience a sense of freedom in creating and that can't be experienced in any other way. Try it today and see what happens – it is a gift waiting to be opened!

I also strongly encourage everyone to expose themselves to some type of instrumental music. The reason that I particularly choose music of this kind is that without words, hearing the music, our inner selves respond in a way that is different than with the various forms of vocal music. Whether that be classical, new age, jazz, it doesn't much matter the genre. What does matter is that you are left to fill in the void with imagination and your own intuitive voice. If this is new to you, be aware that it may take a bit of cultivation to appreciate. If we are used to someone supplying us images, tone, and themes, at first we may feel resistant to filling them in for ourselves. That resistance can range from boredom to irritation, but the important thing is to experiment, enjoy it, and find a non-vocal genre that speaks to you and you to it.

While experiencing or reexperiencing the artistic side of life on a regular basis, make it fun! Think of it as creative play, not just another "to-do"! There are no limitations, no right and wrong answers. If you don't like one thing, try another. If you have never drawn anything in your life, draw something as elementary as a stick figure and recognize even that as awakening the imagination. The main thing is enjoyment —to allow yourself to find inspiration in art, it has to speak to you individually. We have lost our sense of play and falsely think that things have to be "productive" or lead to some end. Let's lose ourselves in the moment, let's play in the sandbox and engage our imaginative energies that resist watching the clock. Now that is true inspiration!

Natural

The second category of inspiration that I encourage you to participate in is natural. This involves consciously putting ourselves in natural settings on a regular basis. Sounds simple, right? How many days have you spent going from the house to the car to the office to the grocery store back to the garage and to the house, only to have gone through the entire day without even as much as 5 full minutes breathing in outside air?? I know I'm guilty.

We need to recognize that as a part of the natural world, our bodies, minds, hearts, and souls long to be engaged with the rest of the outside world. Our feet want to touch the earth, our hands want to touch the soil, our eyes want to take in the gorgeous colors of the sky and earth and water. When we consistently deprive ourselves of this type of inspiration and connection for a long period of time, we start to experience the negative symptoms without even realizing it. When this happens, our perspective gets smaller, less global, we feel less expansive, less generous in spirit, and we get more involved and focused on a smaller range of ideas, issues, and concerns.

Let us open ourselves back up to the whole horizon! Let us breathe in the air, allowing our lungs to be filled, with our arms open wide, and take it all in. I guarantee that if you were to do this daily, standing in your driveway looking at the sky, you would feel a positive difference.

Verbal

This final category involves putting yourself in the path of words that uplift, encourage, and embolden you. Whether you pursue this through prayer or meditation, reading or listening to a book on CD, by taking in these words daily or regularly, you begin the process of continuously overwriting a positive message onto your subconscious and conscious mind. Not only should you make an effort to take these words in, but you should also try and find someone within 24 hours of hearing them, to share them with. The process of taking in positive information is 10 times greater when you repeat it back in some form. They say that the best way to learn something is to become the teacher of it. This is so true! Not only is it good for retention purposes, committing it to long-term memory, but there is something remarkable about hearing your own voice pass the words along to someone else. It is a form of paying it forward. The positive, inspirational effects that the words had on you now become multiplied exponentially by being repeated and taken in by someone else. You have now broadened the ripple in the pond!

The other important element of taking in positive words is that language is the primary vehicle by which thought is communicated. Even when we take in an image, our minds automatically attempt to attach a word label to it. This works backwards as well. If we hear a word, our brains automatically shuffle through the internal rolodex of our experiences and try to attach an image to it so that we can bring it into our framework. This image then links itself to the next image or thought and so on. Imagine the difference between taking in a word like "love" and taking in the word "accident." Something as seemingly harmless as watching the news, actually triggers thoughts and images to become reinforced or dredged up in our minds and that influences the next batch of emotion of thought we create internally. The good news is we have the power to filter out negativity, first and foremost by not putting ourselves in its path. The bad news is we don't always take ownership over this power and we let the world bombard us with whatever it chooses to.

Reading is an excellent way to take in these positive verbal cues. Did you know that there is a direct correlation between how much one reads and what their income level is? Our attitudes and belief systems are heavily influenced by the continuation of the learning, growing process. Even something as seemingly unrelated as our earning capacity is directly impacted by how much we claim power over our intake of positive verbal cues. When we read, we open ourselves up to new ideas, perspectives, and opportunities. Our world expands and along with that, our minds and our spirits.

We greatly increase our likelihood of remaining an active participant in our own recovery plan the more we commit to our own process. Actively seek things out that are going to inspire you, motivate you, and keep you focused on the positive action of today, rather than on negative things that may be running around in your head or reliving things that have happened in the past. Give yourself the best of care and your best self will emerge – not only whole and intact, but even better and stronger than before. Trust that God has your best days yet in front of you!

When I try, I fail. When I
trust, God succeeds.

"The secret of discipline is motivation.
When a man is sufficiently motivated,
discipline will take care of itself."

– SIR ALEXANDER PATERSON

What motivates you to stay in a place of action?
Are you regularly taking in positive
input that motivates you or
negative input that demotivates you?

Present

IV.

How Do You Move Forward?

*Failure is merely an opportunity to
start over again, wiser than before.*

Valor consists in the power of self-recovery.

- EMERSON

My hope is that before you got backed into the "must corner," you faced some of the reality of your situation and cut some of the negative repercussions off at the pass. You may not have, however, and you may have a big mess to figure out. You may not even know how to unravel the mess and that is why you are reading this. Okay, deep breath, let's start from a place of strength and together figure out which end is up.

Step Zero: Pray.

"Prayer begins where human capacity ends."

— MARIAN ANDERSON

I think it is important to point out that this is a continuous and a most important step. The power of prayer cannot be underemphasized. We have a human tendency to forget to pray – to fail to ask for help or praise Him for the gift of this new day. Or to communicate to God at all. For me, prayer never really stopped, but I got lost in the world of self-help and thought if I just dug deep enough, I could find the resources to transform my life on my own, keeping prayer present but on the sideburner. Wrong. It wasn't until my life and everything in it became dedicated in prayer to God, that I truly started my recovery. At the end of this section of the book, you will find a **30-Day Rebounding Devotional** to get you started on the right track. Turning to His Word, spending quiet time contemplating and praying…these are things that are seemingly simple but absolutely critical and amazingly powerful. God is right there. Just a conversation away.

Step One: Write this down:
"With God, I can handle anything
that comes my way."

"As is our confidence, so is our capacity."

– William Hazlitt

Why this statement? Well, to start with it is the Truth. You <u>can</u> handle anything. And I do mean ANYTHING. Even if you are completely broken and broke, unloved, abused, alone, on death's door...with the Lord, you can handle it. And it is very important that you tell yourself that. That you KNOW. Every moment that your self-talk allows you to say, "Can I handle this?" is a momentary hit to your subconscious ability to create the solutions and form a plan for forward action. Change the programming and you change the outcome. You can add whatever you'd like to this statement but don't change the statement itself – try to read it to yourself at least ten times a day during this trying phase of your life. It will help you in ways you won't expect.

Step Two: Assess your situation.
(Whoa, this is a scary step, isn't it?)

*"We win half the battle when we make
up our minds to take the world as we
find it, including the thorns."*

— ORISON S. MARDEN

Assessing the damage involves getting <u>very specific</u> about the circumstances at hand. Taking inventory – whether it be emotional, physical, financial, intellectual, social, or spiritual. Part of the value of this step is it takes a bit of the overwhelm out of the situation, and reduces the drama. No, your entire life is not over. No, your entire future is not doomed. No, you are not entirely a failure. You may have made some choices that led you here, but there isn't anything you can't handle (remember?). Getting really concrete and specific is helpful here. It also reaffirms the fact that you can touch the REALITY of the situation and strip away the emotion for a few moments.

I'm not suggesting that you can stop feeling the emotion, I'm only suggesting that being caught up in the overwhelming emotion of the lack of direction, the fear, and the loss may not serve you every moment in your desire to move forward. Remember, this isn't a process that takes a day or that you are going to whoosh right through as quickly as you read this book. It is an entirely organic and natural process, grieving and recovering, and you can't control the timing entirely. You can choose your actions and perspectives and attitudes, however, and that is what you need to do at this step. Choose to see the specifics, not the generalities of your miserableness. You will be amazed at how that will begin to help you unravel the negative swirl of emotions in the pit of your stomach. I've felt it too.

Step Three: Assess the gap.

"God is in the gaps."

— *Deepak Chopra*

The gap that you are assessing in this step is that space between where you are today and where you'd like to be or need to be. If it is a financial loss that you have experienced, what is the difference between what you are making or have saved today and where you need/want to be on that better day in the future? Looking into this gap and identifying it allows for the first seedlings of creative energy to take root. That creative energy, in the form of ideas, resources, and opportunity is what is eventually going to propel you forward. Don't be too worried about generating a lot of energy at this step (although it will begin to happen naturally, don't be surprised) but let's lay the groundwork for it later on. Tilling the soil, so to speak!

Step Four: Forgive yourself for getting here in the first place.
(This is the step everyone skips but eventually has to visit at some point.)

"Forgiveness is man's deepest need and highest achievement."

— HORACE BUSHNELL

Look, you didn't get here because you were a victim of circumstance. There were actions and choices that led you here. Call this the "tough love" section of the process – the main thing to identify here, however, is despite owning that (and yes, you will eventually have to) you made the best choices you could at the time. Were you actively, consciously making choices that led to the loss of your job, your business, your spouse, your financial security? Of course not, who would do that?! But the bottom line is, sometimes because we are human, our best is not always good enough. Not always good enough to keep us from the brink of disaster and trauma. And, despite that, your primary responsibility to yourself is to LOVE YOURSELF. That includes forgiveness because that love is the UNCONDITIONAL kind. Radical concept, I know, but this is the radically good stuff that God is made of. We have this amazing ability to not let ourselves be human, to only accept perfection, to beat ourselves up constantly with negative self-messages. These tendencies get heightened when we are under the stress of any kind of loss. Pause and breathe. Say to yourself, "I forgive you. I know you did the best you could." When I finally hit this stage, I was a puddle of tears for about two days.

Step Five: Forgive the people that contributed to you getting here.

"To err is Human; to forgive Divine."

—Alexander Pope

Pause. Breathe again. Okay, just like you were doing your best but may have made some choices that didn't lead to all the best outcomes, other people do the same and sometimes they affect us too. How often do you think people actually set out to INTENTIONALLY hurt you? Sure, it happens but in the majority of the circumstances people take actions not knowing ahead of time all of the ramifications and consequences that may result from them. Trust me, the CEO at GM did not intentionally make poor management decisions to make you suffer the pain of losing your job after 23 years of service. Yes, all others are human and fallible too.

You can choose not to forgive them and carry around the hurt, resentment, anger, and sadness. You can even choose to seek vengeance and strike out to hurt them as in "get justice," "teach them a lesson," "show them a thing or two," or just plain, "make them feel the pain." Those are viable choices and people choose them every day. However, I will tell you that these choices will not get you closer to a better day, a better place, or a place of peace and calm inside. Those choices will exacerbate the issues, create more drama, bind you up with more negative emotion, and create a living hell for you. You will expend valuable energy, time, and resources that could have been harnessed in creating your brighter future instead. Your choice. Choose to forgive sooner rather than later and recognize other's weaknesses as you recognize your own humanness and weakness, and you will move forward sooner. You get the picture.

Step Six: Take some small step of action towards a better place.
Baby steps.

*"Well-being is attained little by little,
and is no little thing itself."*

— *Zeno of Citium*

These steps are all relative to where you are today. For some, a good baby step is getting out of bed and taking off the sloppy sweats so they can tackle the day with some modicum of self-respect. For others, a good baby step might be putting together a professional portfolio that outlines their work experiences and skills. There is no point comparing where you are with where someone else is – the comparisons are meaningless. Taking these steps only has meaning in refer-ence to where YOU are today, what YOUR gaps are, what YOU have identified as a good next step. By recognizing this, you are able to practice nonjudgment with yourself and avoid more of that negative self-messaging. There just aren't any rules for this process; the rules are: choose what serves you. If it serves you positively today to eat ice cream and feel the sunshine on your face, then even that could be a good next step – it is whatever moves you closer to a positive place and further from the negative places of fear, paralysis, and self-flagellation.

Step Seven: Talk to someone. Anyone.
(A half hour is okay to whine and vent. A
hour hour a day for a year is not.)

"Everyone needs help from everyone."

– BERTOLT BRECHT

The point here is that it is important to get out of your own head and hear your own voice process the situation at hand. You are not only getting rewarded by having some-one relate to you and where you are (empathically, hope-fully) but you are benefiting in your processing by voicing it out loud. We are not alone – EVER. The only time we are ever really truly alone is when we choose not to connect – and again that is a choice that won't serve us for the bet-ter in every moment. Sure, we all need alone time to think, to pray, to breathe, to be silent, to cry. And then we also need time to not be alone, to meaningfully connect. That is all part of the balance and blend in life and especially in this process.

> "One of the most effective ways in which people can cope with feelings of loneliness is by reframing their loneliness as an active form of solitude. The underlying grief or pain is then seen as having some meaning; it may even be a necessary form of suffering that acts as a transition for further growth. Further, it is important to give yourself hope, realistic expectations that things can and will be better."

> - Dr. Wayne Dyer

Sometimes in our busy lives, we find ourselves surrounded by and interacting with people all day long, having surface-level conversations and trick ourselves into thinking that it is enough. It isn't – we need real, honest human connection with others as much as we need the air we breathe. Honor that and reach out to someone, even in the most difficult moments – it can make all the difference between moving forward and staying stuck. Don't play the waiting game – waiting for someone to notice your pain, your situation, your loneliness. That isn't reasonable – no one is going to take responsibility for your self-care but you. It doesn't mean they don't love you or care – they just aren't on the inside of YOUR experience. You are.

I feel its important to mention here that there are situations where it is entirely appropriate to seek out a professional who is trained to help: a counselor, psychiatrist, grief counselor, doctor, pastor, priest, etc. Sometimes after talking with a friend or family member, it is easier to discern when this next level of care might be appropriate. They are there for a reason. This book is really not designed to be a substitute for qualified mental or emotional care in severe situations. If you suspect there is an abuse, substance use, or any type of mental illness that may be involved in your situation, please reach out for the right help. At the back of this book, you will find some additional resources as well.

Step Eight: Breathe. Let Go.
(No, really...I mean it.)

"If you can't fight, and you can't flee, <u>flow</u>."

– ROBERT ELIOT

It may have been a month that you have felt stuck, or maybe a year. Or maybe longer. It really doesn't matter, because if you have made it to this step, you have already done some tough emotional work and you have created some space and perspective around your situation. You are taking action and that is HUGE. Remember, rebounding is a *verb*, an action. Acknowledge yourself for having gotten here – it is a BIG DEAL. Now, recognize that you can't guarantee any particular outcome for your actions. You remain human, prone to doing your best moment by moment, potentially having that not be good enough to avoid everything negative in life, and will continue to do your best. Recognize that you must continue to forgive yourself. The past has now been put in some kind of a less harsh, judgmental place and it is okay at this stage to let it go. You have potentially sucked all the juicy lessons out of it, and it will propel you forward faster the less you continue to think about it and stay knee-deep in it.

Step Nine: Ask for help if you need it.

*"The healthy and strong individual is the one
who asks for help when he needs it. Whether
he has an abscess on his knee, or in his soul."*

– RONA BARRETT

Wow, I have gotten held up on this step many times myself. In fact, the second time I got pushed into the "must corner" it was because I was too proud and stubborn to ask for help. It was after my divorce and I had my two little babies to care for. I had been temporarily living with my parents until I recovered from the birth and shifted into some semblance of a capable adult. I still felt like a Mac truck had hit my life and wasn't entirely sure what end was up. I knew however, that I wanted to be back out on my own and although I couldn't afford much on my graduate assistant's paycheck, I found a decent apartment near campus, got my brother to co-sign, and was preparing to move in. I didn't, however, have the money for the utility company's deposit and so I put the baby in the car seat and my toddler in the stroller and we went down to Social Services to apply for a hardship grant of $250 to turn on the electricity. I thought I was doing the best I could; I thought I was being resourceful, and I thought I was swallowing my pride! After all, Social Services wasn't exactly where I wanted to be spending my time and since I had recently gone on food stamps I didn't want to be there anymore than I had to. Well, I left that building after getting turned down for the hardship grant, got into my car, and proceeded to get hit by an oncoming car in the intersection just outside of Social Services! Stunned, I got my children out of the car (an 8 year old Volvo I had scraped up $2200 to buy just weeks earlier), made sure everyone was okay and stood on that corner looking at the car, waiting for the police and facing my situation. I can remember the temperature that day and what I was wearing like it was yesterday. I had no other choice in that moment – in that moment I knew I MUST FACE REALITY.

The reality was that I wouldn't have been at Social Services if I just had swallowed my pride and asked my family for help and the $250 for the deposit. I knew I wouldn't have gotten in that car accident if I hadn't been caught up in my own "poor-me" drama in my head and had been paying full attention to that oncoming car in the intersection. It was my own fault I was there standing on that welfare corner, hearing my baby cry, looking at my smashed in, beat up Volvo, feeling dejected that I just got turned down for the grant. When we refuse to ask for help and play the victim, we create more drama to become a victim of! Asking for help when you need it isn't a sign of weakness – it is a sign of strength that we can speak our own needs and get out of own way. Of course, asking for help every other day is a different story altogether.

Step Ten: Be thankful you are right here, right now.

"The only way to live is to accept each minute as an unrepeatable miracle, which is exactly what it is: a miracle and unrepeatable."

– STORM JAMESON

It is easy to be grateful when things are good. When we are at the top of the roller coaster hill, looking down at the beauty that is below and all around us. What is more challenging is to give thanks in the middle of darkness: to recognize the gift of this moment, even if this moment might not be all rose petals and promotions. I promise you, though, although you may not feel it, this moment is perfect and designed for your greater good and it does deserve gratitude and recognition. We'll discuss more about how the up and down cycles of life work together in a later chapter, but for now, let us just be glad that having come this far, we are here to tell about it and we recognize the unique treasure that is contained in this rebounding process, this dynamic active process that allows us to become more conscious of all of our many blessings and choices.

> *There are three kinds of people in the world:*
> *the will's, the won'ts, and the can'ts. The*
> *first accomplish everything, the second oppose*
> *everything, and the third fail in everything.*

> —ANONYMOUS

Which type of person are you?

V.

You are Worth the Best of Care

*"I cannot give the formula for success,
but I can give the formula for
failure – try to please everybody."*

– Herbert B. Swope

Please commit to yourself right now - I mean really commit -
if you haven't already, to taking care of you in the best way
you know how, regardless of what anyone else says or does. If
you have recently lost your job of 23 years, job recruiters may
tell you that what is best for you is to put your resume together and get back on the horse after falling off. You, however,
may have a nagging, sniggling feeling that instead you should
be taking a week off from the world to drive to the ocean and
feel your toes in the sand or going to the movies every day for
a week. Don't underestimate the power of your own internal
intuitive voice! And don't trick yourself into thinking that
just because you aren't taking action that looks progressive to
the outside world that it isn't progressive for you. Go to the
ocean already!!

Very often though, the tough love that we know is best for our children, is exactly the kind of love we need to extend to ourselves. It is the love that separates out every other voice in the world other than the TRUTH. Taking action may not be easy, but oftentimes the very hardest part is seeing through the fog to the real problem at hand and facing the truth for you. You *know* if your actions were part of the problem and you know how to find and create part of the solution. I absolutely believe this about every single individual. We have amazing powers of intuition, honesty, and integrity if we will just allow ourselves to do the real work and strip away the other garbage that stands in our way.

Tough Love Bulls-Eye #1

*You must face your inner need
before you can feel secure.*

The bottom line is, only you know what you truly need. Now, don't get me wrong, sometimes others can have valuable insight and can see things about ourselves that we don't see, such as that we are justifying our own fear by avoiding positive action by playing video games, surfing the net, or watching TV all day...for three straight months. I'm not suggesting that you shut others out of your process, but I am suggesting that you trust yourself and feed yourself: mind, body, and spirit with attention to what is good and useful for you even if that comes in an unusual package that others don't really understand. If you ignore what you really need, you'll always be insecure on some level and seeking it out externally. You'll seek it out in the comfort of food, or alcohol, or entertainment or you'll cling to safe choices and regret not taking bigger risks and chances, knowing that there is more to life. See, intuitively, inside, you already know that you are worth the best and that your security comes from recognizing the incredible, God-created, unique package that is you at your best!

Tough Love Bulls-Eye #2

You can't be a victim <u>and</u> move forward in life.

You are creating a self-fulfilling prophecy when you choose victimhood and project this to everyone around you. We all know people that always seem to tell us their stories about their latest mishaps or tragedies, woes or worries. They have attached their life story to these negative dramas so that they can avoid the real work of living and making choices. It is much easier to remain a victim and blame circumstance, claiming you have no choice. It is harder to take true responsibility and face the reality that we ALWAYS have a choice, that this is what you chose. The problem is, that by avoiding this truth and simultaneously trying to "move forward," you are attempting to lie to yourself. And your inner self knows better. You will always be giving yourself second best, the leftovers, unless you commit to facing the truth.

Tough Love Bulls-Eye #3

You are what you think about.

Look, if you always think about sickness or need, you are going to experience sickness or need. Try this: observe your thoughts for a full day and make a note of whether or not your thoughts are reflective of what you've already experienced, what you are experiencing now, or what you want to achieve. Try and assess how much of the time you are allowing your thoughts to support positive forward movement, rebounding you into a better space, or how much of the time you are allowing your thoughts to bring up fear, self-doubt, thoughts about need (not having enough money or love are the big ones, usually), or staying in your comfortable "discomfort" zone. There is no rocket science here – change your thoughts, and change your life!

Find a spot to sit comfortably and try the following visualization exercise:

Relax and breathe. Close your eyes…picture yourself at the edge of a beautiful, dense forest. You feel curious and excited, you know inside that you are entering a new world and you can't wait to step into it…there is a slightly worn area in the grass beneath your feet and you notice that it forms a little path leading you into the woods. You begin to follow the path. As you enter, your heart quickens and there is a mixture of excitement and fear. As you walk into the trees, your eyes adjust to the shady, cool forest and you can smell the woodsy, earthy smell and feel a slight breeze blowing through the trees. You continue walking, realizing that the forest wasn't as deep as you thought and a clearing ahead appears… you wonder what is up there. Will you see animals? Will there be warm sunlight? You let your imagination roam for a moment and you imagine what you might see there…

This exercise only takes a few moments but it puts you in imagination mode and engages your senses in creating the scenery of a new world in your mind. Every idea, every journey, every accomplishment began with an imaginative thought! We all have a remarkable muscle that we can flex any old time we want to! What new life circumstances could you create through your imagination?

Tough Love Bulls-Eye #4

When you choose fear and inaction, you choose automatic self-limitation.

"Jump and a net will appear."

– SALLY HOGSHEAD

This goes hand in hand with #3, doesn't it? We can't know what is going to happen when we take an action, but we do know that by not taking the action, nothing will happen and we will keep getting what we've gotten. I mean, what do you have to lose by trying? Break it down here – write it down. What <u>specifically</u> are you afraid of losing by taking the action, making the choice? I love to play the "worst case scenario" game with myself all the time – take that specific fear and assume it comes true – then what? Say I am afraid to make the "wrong" choice and take the job I really want and looks more fun? What happens when I lose that other opportunity? So, I can't go back and do it over – so what? Won't there be new information, new perspective, new contacts, and new opportunities for me on the other side? Yes, there will! More often than not, we create regrets in our lives by not taking action and wondering what would have happened "if" rather than the other way around. This is your best life, your LIFE we are talking about. Its the only one we have to live this time around, in this form – go on, take a chance…You are worth it!!

While coaching individuals, there is usually a moment in which they realize that fear is holding them back from taking some action that would ultimately propel them forward. When I look into their eyes and tell them very honestly that they owe themselves the very best life, that they are worth taking a chance on, many times I see brimming emotion come up immediately. They look at me with a question mark in their eyes, daring to hope that maybe I am showing them the truth after perhaps years of subconsciously acting as if they weren't worth it…and regardless of position or title or status, it happens just the same. In this moment I am reminded how terribly vulnerable we all are, underneath all the stories, all the circumstances, all the bravado it took to get us where we are. We are all incredibly connected and raw to the power of our own potential and we have a remarkable daily opportunity to embrace THIS moment, be grateful for it, and create with it something precious if we only allow ourselves to imagine and feel and act.

*"It is hard to fail, but it is worse
never to have tried to succeed."*

— THEODORE ROOSEVELT

*"Ninety-nine percent of failures come
from people who have the habit of
making excuses."*

— GEORGE WASHINGTON CARVER

What are your excuses? What
have you failed to try?

VI.

Grieving our Losses

"Blessed are those who mourn,
for they will be comforted."

- *MATTHEW 5:4*

This is the point in the journey, where you get to start telling your story. Turning your mess into a message of hope for others going through something similar may seem far off right now, but regardless, you putting a voice to your experience, not just hearing mine, is really important to me. What happened in your life that is forcing you to rebound?

Grieving is a natural part of our human experience and cannot be forced into a box of any kind. Each person's journey and experience of it is as individual as the person themselves. The hope that is given to us in a true relationship with God and His son, Jesus, is that this grieving we are experiencing is here for a season, and like all seasons, will pass through and open up to a new day at some point. There are some "tough love" references in this book, but that is never to replace empathy or compassion. God calls on us to be compassionate and loving with others, as we would be with ourselves. Voicing what happened to you, is a way of extending that compassion to yourself and honoring your story.

Many times, until we have done this, we carry shame around our story. Voicing our experience doesn't make that shame instantly go away but it acts as a sort of release and allows us to begin healing. Shame is the most devastating and negative of human emotions. It can literally stop us in our tracks, eliminating the ability to take inspired action, or sometimes any action at all. When I lost my business in Raleigh, one of the reasons I had a hard time recovering financially was I was too ashamed to go back to old employers or network in my old circles. I felt as if everyone would see me as a failure, so why would they have confidence enough in me to hire me or help me get back into business for myself? The shame was paralyzing. What I realized many years later, was that I was much more invested and aware of my story than they were – they had moved on with their lives and were caught up in their own challenges and concerns of the day. The last thing on their mind was what had happened to me.

I also carried a lot of shame around having been divorced twice. Once was devastating enough – how on earth do I rebound from this again? Would anyone seriously ever want to date me or share their life with me? I felt like a loser, honestly. Having grown up Catholic, divorce was seen as a reason to separate you from God, literally causing you to be excluded from portions of a church service or even be told you are no longer welcome. It wasn't until years later, after going to a Catholic priest to confess my shame around it and voice my grieving around it, that I was pardoned, released from my internal burden of self-depreciation and judgment. I had been carrying it for many years but in reality, I could have laid that burden down at any point – God was ready for me to experience joy and love, not shame and anger at myself. What burdens are you carrying?

Relationships

Divorce, death of a loved one, and abusive situations are among the most common sources of trauma and loss that people experience. Getting back up after being knocked down by any of these experiences can take years or sometimes even a lifetime. I met my husband Kelley only five months after the death of his teenage son, due to a tragic suicide. Despite my many setbacks, I had never experienced the loss of someone that close to me and walking alongside his journey these past three and half years has created an even deeper compassion and depth of understanding in me. Losses like these rock you to your core – you are never the same afterwards. There is nothing anyone can say that will make these losses less painful, but I hope you know you are not alone. Not only is God always by your side but there are many other people grieving in this season with you.

I want to encourage you to take a moment and record some of your relationship losses and experiences here.

_____
_____
_____
_____
_____
_____
_____
_____
_____
_____
_____
_____
_____
_____

Money

I am going to speak specifically about financial recovery for a moment because at this time in our history there are so many families and individuals suffering from severe financial setbacks and hardships. It ranks right up there with sickness, death of a loved one, and divorce as the biggest causes of stress in our lives and it can be profound in its consequences.

It hits us on personal and professional levels that we never thought possible because it questions our ability to make our way in the world and provide for ourselves, one of our deepest sources of security and safety. Without money we have no home, no belongings, nothing to show for ourselves. We are left with a raw version of our own vulnerability because it directly speaks to our ability, our personal judgment. If a loved one gets sick and dies, so much of that is out of our control that it doesn't necessarily hit the spots closest to the guilt and self-blame centers of our inner selves.

Financial loss, however, seems to be all about us. Where did we go wrong? What choices should we have made differently? Why didn't we cash out sooner? Why didn't we see it coming? Why can't I get the job that I deserve? Why can't I manage my money better? Why, Why, Why and Why? The could'ves, should'ves, and would'ves move into our psyche and they don't let us go. Because of this, I think that it is one of the hardest to recover from emotionally. We are so very hard on ourselves.

Take a moment here to talk about your financial story of loss.

_____

_____

_____

_____

_____

_____

_____

Health

When health challenges strike, it is very difficult to compartmentalize it and have it not effect every area of our life. When my own body shut down due to stress, there were days that it hurt to go outside, days it hurt to have my clothing touch my skin. Even if you are recovered from your illness now, the threat of something similar returning always haunts you as well. We learn very quickly not to take a moment of feeling good for granted. But injury, disease, chronic conditions, addictions...these are not easy to rebound from. We grieve the loss of freedom, choice, activity, joy, functionality, and even connectedness to others. Many times we can get trapped in the feeling that "no one understands what I'm going through" and it can become a serious wedge in our communication with others.

Start here by telling your story.

_____

_____

_____

_____

_____

_____

_____

_____

_____

_____

Acts of God

This may seem like a strange category to explore, but many people experience losses around natural disasters, accidents, weather events, civil unrest, or situations way beyond the realm of their control. When I was 17 years old, I was in a serious car accident when I hit a deer that was flying across the freeway in the beginning of November in Michigan. The large, 10-point buck that I hit was killed instantly on impact and the roof of my car was peeled back as he slid across the roof, only inches from my head. An officer on the scene afterwards marveled at the fact that aside from glass from the shattered windshield all over me I was still alive and well. He called it an "Act of God" accident, since no one except God apparently had any control over the deer or the chain of events that occurred to cause the accident. Still to this day, I cannot drive down a dark road without having my eyes almost glued to the passenger side mirror, exactly where that deer hit me. For almost a year after that, I couldn't drive at night at all without shaking and feeling my heart beat out of my chest in fear.

Hurricanes and tornadoes are common east coast disasters that cause large scale devastation in their wake. Recovering from the losses of these incidents can be staggering. Where do you even begin? Even upon this writing, Hurricane Patricia was scheduled to hit the Mexican coastline, one of the strongest storms ever recorded in human history. How do you rebound from events like these?

Record some of the circumstances in your story here:

_____

_____

_____

_____

_____

_____

_____

_____

_____

_____

_____

_____

_____

_____

_____

_____

_____

_____

_____

_____

_____

_____

_____

_____

_____

If you'd like to share your story with me privately or you'd like to share it publically, there are options for doing that. I'd love to hear your story so that I can pray for your recovery and your journey specifically. Visit *theresabassett.com* and Click the "Share Your Story" button. You can also visit the *Rebounding Revolution* Facebook page and share your story with others so that a wider community may pray with you and offer support.

> *"Praise be to the God and Father of our Lord Jesus Christ, the Father of compassion and the God of all comfort, who comforts us in all our troubles, so that we can comfort those in any trouble with the comfort we ourselves receive from God."*

> *-2 Corinthians 1:3-4*

VII.

Up and Down Cycles: Working Together for Good

"We have come to fear failure too much.
Failure is the practice essential for success."

— CHARLES F. KETTERING

What initiates the up cycles in our lives? Something specific can happen to trigger this positive chain or we can choose (gee, that word comes up an awful lot) to create it in our own lives. I overheard a personal trainer at the gym on day telling her client, "You are always only one workout away from feeling better!" Could it really be that easy?

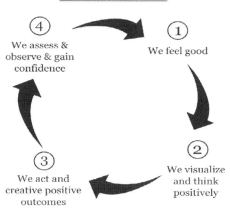

THE UP CYCLE

(4) We assess & observe & gain confidence

(1) We feel good

(2) We visualize and think positively

(3) We act and creative positive outcomes

Well, yes, sometimes it can if we've already done some of the heavy lifting, some of the ongoing self-care, forgiveness, and healing work. If we have a bunch of garbage in our lives, our psyche, and our relationships, however, it could be more complicated too. That is why the 21-Day Rebounding Radical Action Plan works (visit *theresabassett.com* for your free download) – by addressing many these potential sticking points <u>simultaneously</u>, beginning the process of forming new habits, and encouraging the perpetuation of The Up Cycle.

When you really know you have arrived, however, is when you realize that the up AND down cycles work together for your good. The Down Cycle looks like this:

THE DOWN CYCLE

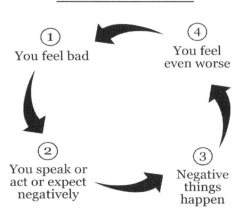

Eventually the Down Cycle leads to places no one likes talking about. If it is left unchecked (you'll sometimes hear it referred to as the "negative spiral" for this reason) – depression, illness, addictions, neurosis, even suicide – can be the result. Extreme down cycles that are never addressed and are left to claim power over the individual's life. Sometimes that happens because when we're in it, we can't see it for what it is – the emotions are too all-encompassing.

That is part of the reason I suggest here that you don't wait until you feel better to begin doing something about your situation. You may not be able to see the forest for the trees and how badly you are stuck in a down cycle. So don't wait, remember that ACTION <u>PRECEDES</u> FEELING and begin taking some kind of action today. Life is simply too short and too precious to be lived stuck in a negative down cycle. We are missing out on the love, the joy, the fun, and the abundance we were designed to experience in the full expression of living!

However, without The Down Cycle we can't appreciate its opposite – we don't get to reach down deep and decide what kind of stuff we're really made of if we stay perpetually in an Up Cycle. Those character-building, fork-in-the-road moments in the down cycle are needed to become whole, develop depth and true gratitude, and ultimately reach our potential. Can you see now how both of the cycles work together for your good?

According to Michael Lewis, this is why "Children enjoy a technological advantage over adults...they haven't sunk a lot of psychological capital into a particular self," states Lewis in his book, *Next*. "When a technology comes along that rewards people who are willing to chuck overboard their old selves for the new ones - and it isn't just the Internet that does this...the people who aren't as invested in their old selves have an edge." It goes on to discuss how there is no story to drag young minds down from the process of re-recreation and if there are older people willing to become unchained from their old story, it is because they have had a health scare or are on death's door! All of the previous limitations become meaningless and risk is once again acceptable, opening up all new possibilities. The Up Cycle is thus initiated.

When creating the movie of our lives, whereby we are the writer, actor, and director of our own created script, we always have an opportunity to use every cycle, every new day, and every choice as an initiation of The Up Cycle. Even the things that seemingly appear horrible or tragic on the surface can represent a growing or learning opportunity, a character-shaping moment. The challenge then becomes seeing The Up and Down cycles, the yin and the yang, as complementary, both working together to make us whole and fully actualized in our potential.

At one point, the script of my life's movie had me cast as a community college teacher, teaching humanities and critical thinking, which I loved. I thrived on the stimulation of the discussions inside the classroom, the thrill of watching adult learning take place when someone would have an "aha" moment. What I didn't thrive on so much was repeatedly staying up until 1 a.m. grading papers or preparing lessons with a newborn nursing on me and getting a paycheck at the end of the month that left me sorely short of the making-ends-meet mark. One day, my home's electric got turned off and I suddenly found myself backed into the "must face it" corner. I had to take a really hard look at what was serving me in the current situation and what clearly wasn't. I had to write a new story so that I could provide for my children and my own sleep and wellness needs. As an English graduate school student, I didn't have a highly lucrative job market to tap into. I also had small children and was a single parent, which meant that I had a lot of child-care and schedule concerns. What on earth was the next twist in this movie going to look like?

I already knew I could communicate and that I loved people. I remembered my father telling me for years that I should go into sales, that I would be great at sales. After years of waving off his suggestion as not lofty enough for my ideals, I was ready to try anything that didn't compromise my core values. I had to make more money for my children! I had a strong personal "why" and with my back in the corner, I knew I had to be completely open in order to create a different reality. A job ad for a car sales job was the first and only ad I responded to the very next day and lined up an interview that afternoon. Car dealerships, I learned, were probably some of the easiest places to get a sales job as the turnover was so high. So yes, of course I got the job and was on my way to selling Chevy's that day – a dramatic shift from teaching critical thinking and English! That one decision put me a on a lucrative path to a sales career I loved in real estate sales that I would never have been open to under normal circumstances. My movie now had a surprising plot twist and I had unearthed a whole new range of talents and gifts in myself as the star that I had no idea existed in me.

See, if we choose to take off the blinders and create new habits, we can throw out the old script, the one where we cast ourselves as victims of circumstance, and create a new script. We *can* rebound. And powerfully! And not just once – over and over again so that we are continuously dying to old parts of us that no longer serve us and keep us from getting where we want to go, being reborn to the new possibilities that exist in front of us. Is that a gift, or what??! That is crazy exciting to me!

*"The men who try to do something and fail
are infinitely better than those who try
and do nothing and succeed."*

— LLOYD JAMES

Are you actively participating in or creating an up cycle or a down cycle right now?
What is the next plot twist in the movie of your life?

The 30-Day
Rebounding Revolution
Devotional

DAY 1

Start Where You Are At

"For I know the thoughts that I think toward you, saith the Lord, thoughts of peace, and not of evil, to give you an expected end. Then ye shall seek me, and find *me*, when ye shall search for me with all your heart."

JEREMIAH 29:11-13

Ahh…just breathe. A new beginning. A fresh start. Each day is such an amazing blank canvas to paint a new picture of our lives on. Today, we embrace this together. God grants us unbelievable grace and beauty daily in the morning of a new day. Today of all days, Day 1, represents a morning in your life, the dawn of a new remarkable day. Breathe into this moment, right where you are at. Wide open spaces lie in front of us for renewal, rebirth, regrowth. Let us pray for the wisdom to see those spaces…

God, please grant me courage and peace today – the courage to face what IS and the peace in knowing that you have something so much better in store for me. Reach into my heaped up heart and carry the weight of my grieving for this day so that I may breathe into it easy and lighter than before. Lord, you alone have the ability to infuse your amazing brand of unconditional Love into my life and help me create a new life through the allowing of Your will for me to unfold perfectly. With the power of the Holy Spirit you whisper Your words of Love and light into my ears and I receive them today, this morning, this dawn in my life. Thank you, Lord, for allowing me to find you today and hope in a new better day in front of me.

Thank you, thank you, thank you for allowing me to live into this prayer today.

DAY 2

No Judgment

**"Praise the Lord, O my soul; all my
inmost being, praise his holy name.
Praise the Lord, O my soul, and
forget not all his benefits – who
forgives all your sins and heals
all your diseases, who redeems
your life from the pit and crowns
you with love and compassion,
who satisfies your desires with
good things so that your youth
is renewed like the eagle's."**

PSALM 103: 1-5

So often we are our own worst enemies. We blame
ourselves, going around and around in our heads saying things like, "If I had just not….", "If only I had….",
These words of self-judgment hurt us on so many levels, internally we are hardly able to look at ourselves
in the eyes, only to see our past failures and disap-
pointments. We fail to see anything positive, to grace

ourselves any patience or understanding, choosing instead to only look at what is missing, broken, falling short. Today, even if only for one day, let us start learning how to change that choice. Today, let us choose to see what is good, pure, and redeeming, allowing those things to be acknowledged so that we can raise our eyes and see something new. There is so much more available to us if we can slowly learn to make this different choice.

> *Dearest God, I pray that you absolve me and wash me clean of the need to beat up on myself today. Lift my eyes to something different and new so that I can instead see the imperfect perfection you have placed inside of me and my life. Lead me to a new understanding so that I may look back not with judgment but with peace, knowing that Your will has unfolded in my life and has shaped my journey in a remarkable beautiful way. Lord, help me see my challenges and disappointments as opportunities to get closer to you and learn to lean into Your grace and strength. I pray you humble my heart so that I understand that You alone have the power to point out right action and that in the future I continue to willingly submit and listen to the direction you place in my heart. Place*

in me an understanding that ultimately I am only responsible for this and with Your Love I may begin to grant myself unconditional Love through my relationship with You.

Thank you, thank you, thank you for allowing me to live into this prayer today.

DAY 3

Removing the Ceiling

**"Commit to the Lord whatever you
do, and your plans will succeed."**

PROVERBS 16:3

Without even realizing it we oftentimes create limits on what is possible in our lives. But with God in
our lives, by putting His unconditional Love for us at
the center, there are no limits that exist. The truest
desires of our heart are placed there with the undilut-
ed, irrepressible knowledge that they are reachable.
When we love from the purest place possible we are
tapping into a river of source energy that God alone
represents. Today, let us tap into that wellspring of
joy and knowing, throwing open the floodgates and
any artificial barriers or limitations we have placed in
our lives. Let us open our lives to God and watch the
amazing unfolding that is possible.

*Dear Lord, show me today how to love you
without limits and receive your Love without
the need to box it in in any way. I ask that*

you show me how to invite in the ease and grace that is possible through You. I bow my head to you in recognition that even my wildest dreams pale in comparison to the fullness of life that you offer through You. Thank you, thank you, thank you for blessing me with the wisdom to ask for Your guidance and help me remove my own limited ideas and barriers, submitting myself to the knowledge that the river of Love that is available through you is so much more refreshing and bountiful.

Thank you, thank you, thank you for allowing me to live into this prayer today.

DAY 4

Grant Yourself Grace

"Humble yourselves, therefore, under God's mighty hand, that he may lift you up in due time. Cast all your anxiety on him because he cares for you."

1 Peter 5: 6-7

Today is the day to be easy on yourself, restore resources, add resources. Whatever happened in the past is exactly that...past. Let it go, bless and release it. Allow the grace that you extend to yourself today to create a blueprint for a new pattern - a pattern that supports you and builds you stronger rather than tearing you down. Sinking down into your own wonderful body, thank yourself for showing up for yourself today and take a nice deep breath in...exhale. Even if the past is a poor representation of what you are capable of, disallow that to define you now. Only you carry that negative labeling forward and only you have the ability to hand it over to God and allow in something kinder, gentler, and more empowering. Being a good steward of the gifts you have been given in your life means beginning with an acknowledgement that there are gifts INSIDE you. How can you create a new pattern of grace today?

> *Dear God, please help me extend your grace to myself today and breathe into this next new chapter with a sense of renewal. Help me release the past anxieties, fears, and disappointments that have bound me and usher in a new era, a better day. Fill me with your Love today, infusing my spirit with your most Holy Spirit. Lord, take my worries and previous grievances and give me new eyes to see with, new ears to hear your word and your will being spoken into my life.*
>
> *Thank you, thank you, thank you for allowing me to live into this prayer today.*

DAY 5

Dive Deep

**"Remain in me, and I will remain
in you. No branch can bear fruit
by itself; it must remain in the
vine. Neither can you bear fruit
unless you remain in me. I am the
vine, you are the branches. If a
man remains in me and I in him,
he will bear much fruit; apart
from me you can do nothing."**

JOHN 15: 4-5

An object in motion tends to stay in motion whereas
an object at rest tends to stay at rest. Today, let us
focus on the powers of momentum and how very far
that wave can carry us. Diving deep requires that we
play "all in," that we give our lives the benefit not only
of the doubt but of our full engagement. Holding
ourselves back actually requires more effort than our
100% participation, whether we are cognizant of it
or not. Ever had a "kid in the sandbox" experience,

where time literally fails to be recognized, you are so swept up in the current moment that everything else falls away? Today, let us welcome that energy into our worlds and give our lives our full attention, RIGHT NOW. Diving deep only requires that we trust that in this current state all is perfect and the wave of our willingness to engage will carry us perfectly to the next moment as well.

Today I pray, Lord, that you allow me to jump in and be perfectly willing to get messy and engage in this beautiful imperfect life you have granted me. Let me not be afraid but rather be empowered, resting easy in the knowledge that you are always walking in front of me to clear the path for what is best for me. God, grant me the ability to put fear aside and engage fully, whole heart in.

Thank you, thank you, thank you for allowing me to live into this prayer today.

DAY 6

Get Moving

**"In his heart a man plans his course,
but the Lord determines his steps."**

PROVERBS 16:9

What are you waiting for? Something to hit you over the head and say "Get going"? Okay, this is your wake up call day then…get going already! Every day that you think of the action but stand in a lack of willingness to take the action is just another day that you become more and more disassociated with your own power. God gave us the amazing gift of free will, the ability to either choose something that moves us closer into the Truth with Him or further away. Does standing in a static place move you closer or further away? Inertia is typically dictated by fear – very often fear of the unknown. Do you know what is right around the corner?? No! Why assume, however, that it is scary? God blesses us through right ACTION, not inaction. Take a step, make a move, get going and get growing…right now. God will bless you for it.

Dear Lord, please gift me the proper motivation, willingness, and courage to step out in action today in order that I may more fully embrace this life you have blessed me with. Place me the spirit of fearlessness that makes taking action easier, more natural, than standing still. God guide my hands and my feet with direction and guidance so that I may more closely walk in step with you today.

Thank you, thank you, thank you for allowing me to live into this prayer today.

DAY 7

Rest

**And on the seventh day God ended
his work which he had made; and
he rested on the seventh day from
all his work which he had made.**

GENESIS 1:27-28

Wow, a big start to a brand new chapter. You have
come so far in the past seven days that today dic-
tates a need for a breather. Let us stop today and
celebrate a meaningful pause. Resting periodically is
as valuable as the inspired action we focused on just
yesterday. It is resting that we allow healing to oc-
cur, replenishing and rebuilding to happen at even a
cellular level. Our hearts, our minds, and our bodies
need and crave deep down rest. In this busy busy
world we are so often driven to the edge of our capacity, today we recognize and celebrate our need
for full-on stopping, allowing the ebbs to become as
valuable a part of our rebounding as the flows.

God, thank you so much for my need for rest. Help me recognize that honoring this need will only bring me closer to you, give me an even greater ability to hear you speak to my heart, and open my life up to the nourishing your Love offers daily. Let me see this need as a strength not a weakness as I become more and more willing to acknowledge how it all works together perfectly for my greater good.

Thank you, thank you, thank you for allowing me to live into this prayer today.

DAY 8

Wander with Wonder

**"And we know that in all things
God works for the good of
those who love him, who have
been called to his purpose."**

ROMANS 8:28

Every day…yes, even THIS day, has the potential of being full of amazement. What will this day offer you? What lies right around the corner of even the next hour? Do you remember the last time you felt like a little kid on Christmas morning, running down the steps to see what was waiting under the tree for you? Today, let us embrace the wonder of each ordinary moment as holding the potential for the extraordinary. Join me in letting an open-ended question "what if….?" guide us throughout the day and lead us into the world of potentialities, beyond the mere mundane.

Dearest Lord, today grant me the ability to be amazed, truly in awe of the possibilities you have placed all around me in my life. Let me remove my human limitations and soak myself in wonder, letting it seep into my pores and transport me to a different space all together. I pray, God, that you open my eyes in childlike appreciation for each and every moment and the mystery it contains.

Thank you, thank you, thank you for allowing me to live into this prayer today.

DAY 9

Practice Positive Expectancy

**"Now the God of hope fills you
with all joy and peace in believing,
that ye may abound in hope."**

Romans 15:13

Look into your heart today and ask yourself truthfully what you are expecting to see in front of you. Do you look forward to experiencing the very best or do you constantly inject the energy of fear, anxiety, lack, and settling for something lesser into the future? What we look for, we find. Our reality mirrors our perspective but it is no accident…for in fact, it is our perspective that even shapes and co-creates our reality. God gifts us free will so that we continuously have the choice in front of us to embrace heaven or hell. Do we choose to experience joy and abundance, expecting more of the same, or do we opt for something far less than that promise of fulfillment? Today, let us flex the muscle of absolute positive expectancy.

God, show me today how to hold a brighter place of expectation at the front of my vision for the future. Shine your light into the darkest corners of my imagination and bring new life to old spaces. Help me expect only the best as the natural outcome of your promise to provide everlasting life through you. Keep me and guide me so that that level of positivity becomes a natural extension of who I am in my daily walk with you, Lord.

Thank you, thank you, thank you for allowing me to live into this prayer today.

DAY 10

Every Day Matters

**"Fulfill your works,
your daily tasks."**

EXODUS 5:13

Today let us remember that each and every day makes a difference. Watching people move through their lives on autopilot, with an air of complacency, even apathy, reminds us today that in many ways it is the ultimate way to show ingratitude and take the day we have in front of us completely for granted. Each day is a gift of the highest caliber – it is truly something to be cherished and valued. Not recognizing that, sliding through, living by the law of minimal effort, puts us in a disempowered position that ultimately leads to an emotional, mental, and spiritual laziness. God has opened every day to us an opportunity for growth. Let us be mindful and present for that daily gift and be good stewards of our time resources.

*God, please grant me the wisdom and
discernment to see where I can make good*

use of my time today and have an attitude of gratitude for every moment you have gifted me. Breathe appreciation into my every move so that I may glorify your name in my daily actions and words. Help me see that each and every day is an amazing gift that is not to be squandered and wasted but rather one to be held close and protected like the finest diamond.

Thank you, thank you, thank you for allowing me to live into this prayer today.

DAY 11

No Attachments

"Here am I; send me."

Isaiah 6:8

Stepping out in faith does not mean that you have to "figure it out." The Lord clears a path before you and allows you to rest in faith and trust. Doing that, however, means that you have to be willing to let go of your attachment to what it all looks like. You may think that you know what your life looks like when it is all "fixed," but God may have a completely different plan in mind for you. Being able to walk in His presence means that you can let God take the steering wheel and while being an active participant by stepping out in inspired action and faith, does not mean that you have to have the way all mapped out. Letting go of our attachments is not easy and means that we must humble ourselves to God's ultimate wisdom. How many times do we as parents decide for something on our children's behalf only to be questioned: "But WHY, Mom?" "Because I said so" is often the answer but what is really built into that statement is a whole load of reasons we don't necessarily want to take an hour to explain or expound upon to our children. What we are really saying is "TRUST ME" and my experience for I have your best interest at heart. Lovingly, our Father also holds us in the palm of His hand and calls us to trust upon Him and let go of our attachment to always understanding His logic and reasons for it all. Breathe into letting go of these attachments today.

Dear Lord, help me trust and understand that you always have my best at heart and your reasons go way beyond my understanding. Place in me the ability to hear your Truth and trust it will always lead me in the right directions in the right timing. Help me always see the good in every situation and circumstance as you have designed me to see. I know that once this capacity is developed in me, I will know the unconditional nature of your love for me and be able to see your abundance written all over my life.

Thank you, thank you, thank you for allowing me to live into this prayer today.

DAY 12

Pay Attention

**Trust in the Lord with all your
heart and lean not on your own
understanding; in all your ways
acknowledge him, and he will
make your paths straight.**

Proverbs 3:5-6

Watch and listen. Watch and listen. Every day lives provide opportunities for growth and learning all around
us. The spirit of overcoming calls us to breathe into new
possibilities every single new day. Just as ceaseless
as the ocean rolling into the shore is God ceaselessly
offering us chances for abundance and redemption.
People, places, conversations, references to resources…they pass along our paths all day long. Open
your eyes and ears today to the absolute grace that is
all around you! You are surrounded by creative energy, the energy of life pulsating at your very doorstep.
When you look out your window what do you see?
Trees, grass emerging forth with new buds, leaves,

blades reaching up to the sun. In winter, perhaps snow blanketing the ground allowing life beneath the surface to be deeply nourished in slumber. Your neighbors have stories, life wisdom…open yourself up to learning about them. Pick up the phone and re-connect with a friend and truly listen. Are you being offered an opportunity to be in service to someone else today in some way? Is there a door to open for someone? A chance to listen with a compassionate heart? God offers us every day miracles in every single thing around us…His abundance is staggering!! Pay attention! Put on opportunity-colored glasses and see the world which He truly created for you, always reaching for goodness and growth. Participate in the world's recovery and progress today.

Dearest Lord, I am here as your servant. Heighten my senses, increase the strength of my opportunity radar so that I can easily see the ways you wish me to be of service to those around me today. Help me look beyond my own worries, concerns, and agendas and understand there is something you have in store for me that goes so much further and reaches so many others. Make me a beacon of light and hope for others today, so that they may see your love shining through me. Place a cheerful willingness in me, God, so that these moments are seen and effortlessly seized as your Spirit moves in and through me.

Thank you, thank you, thank you for allowing me to live into this prayer today.

DAY 13

Are We There Yet?

**"Do not be anxious about anything,
but in everything, by prayer and
petition, with thanksgiving, present
your requests to God. And the
peace of God, which transcends
all understanding, will guard
your hearts and your minds."**

PHILLIPIANS 4:6-7

The journey, we hear…it is about the journey not the
destination. So easy to hear and so hard to live! In
our culture of survival of the fittest, we are subconsciously programmed into the delusion that there is
some end result or state of arrival that "makes it all
better." Today is it. THIS day is the day for your
rebirth, your revival! Just as the sun rises every day
over the ocean, asking not continuously if it is time
to set yet, we too must sink into this PRESENT moment and arrive right here and right now. Embrace
what we ARE. Be worthy of the abundance around

us right now by practicing our eyes to see it, our ears to hear it.

Just as children clamoring in the back seat of the car on a long road trip, we sit all day, checking our bank balances to see if we have "enough" yet only to be disappointed that indeed we do not. We fight over the map so that we mark out the route, counting the mile markers to each exit, excited that we are "getting closer." Striving in this way means that we are cutting ourselves off from what is available to us right now. As children we can't see yet that just sitting in the car with our sister or brother, laughing and joking at the last funny sign or license plate we just passed is a memory to cherish forever. One day sister or brother might not be there right beside us to treasure. Looking at the back of our parent's necks, listening to them chat or whistle to the radio or tell goofy jokes or even complain about their legs aching from the journey…all these things alone are precious in and of themselves. Allow what is around you right now to delight you. Step back for a moment and be an observer…what have you been missing along the journey in your focus on some illusionary destination? What is right in front of you to appreciate?

Dear God, I ask you for the ability to be fully present for me life today. Please work in me to create the appreciation for who you have made me to be, the gifts that are already present in me and in my life, so that I can truly BE. I know you have created me in your image and I trust that this image, while growing and evolving, is also perfect as it IS today. I pray today that you help me feel that appreciation and gratitude. Help me reach inside and touch all the good, the highest vision for me, that you have placed in my life and in my being at this very moment in time.

Thank you, thank you, thank you for allowing me to live into this prayer today.

DAY 14

To Forgive Divine

**"Come to me, all you who are
weary and burdened, and I will
give you rest. Take my yoke
upon you and learn from me,
for I am gentle and humble in
heart, and you will find rest
for your souls. For my yoke is
easy and my burden is light."**

MATTHEW 11: 28-30

What is more difficult forgiving others or forgiving ourselves? Did we take actions that led to negative consequences? Often times we are playing the "shoulda, woulda, coulda" game against ourselves. God alone offers us Divine forgiveness and a model of what we need to extend to others and first, and foremost, to ourselves. No, we are not perfect but we are perfect in our imperfection. Free will is offered to us so that we might learn how to make good choices, so that we can participate in co-creating heaven or hell in our lives every day. Along with that awesome right comes an awesome responsibility. As He extends a pure unconditional love to us we too are called to extend that to ourselves. And forgiveness is a huge part of what that means.

Determine that today you are ready to let go of carrying the crosses that you carry against yourself or others. He already carried that burden for us and even in our condemnation of Him, He forgave us. There is nothing, absolutely nothing, that seperates you from His Love if you so choose to accept it. You are forgiven every action, every transgression. Choose life today. Choose something so much lighter than carrying around grudges and victimization. Choose to unburden yourself today and love and forgive unconditionally. It is the greatest gift you could give yourself. New life begins on the other side of that forgiveness.

> *Dear Lord, you have given us the ultimate gift of absolution and forgiveness. Help me extend that to the people in my life that have hurt me in the past. Help me also extend that beautiful expression of unconditional love to myself. Place in me a compassion and an amazing, miraculous empathy so that I can allow you to truly wipe the slate of the past clean and bring me into a new life. By*

carrying forward old grudges, old regrets, old feelings of being a victim I understand that I am allowing myself to be separated from the peace and love that is available to me. I ask that you help me lay those down today so that I can step forward a new person, renewed in faith, renewed in love.

Thank you, thank you, thank you for allowing me to live into this prayer today.

DAY 15
Raise the Bar

**"I am the Lord, the God of
all mankind. Is anything
too hard for me?"**

*Jeremiah **32:27***

What are you accepting in your life that is substandard? If God planted greatness in you, and trust me He has planted in every single one of us, what are you allowing in your life as your "reality" that needs to be upgraded? Are your circumstances dictating how you feel about your life and your self? In God's eyes we are perfect and worthy of truly allowing ourselves to feel worthy of the very best of care. Often times, an internal lack of self worth can lead us into self-defeating behaviors that move us in a direction very different that that best care. Overeating, overdrinking, overanalyzing, overjudging, overescaping…these are all forms of actions that are signs that somewhere along the line we bought a bill of goods that said we weren't worth more. Rise up today in your opinion of what you are worth! Straighten your shoulders, raise your head high and claim something better!

Decide today that it is a new day for raising the bar. Examine your life and shine a loving flashlight into the dark corners of your actions, thoughts, and words. What needs to be lifted up? Choose that today is the day for more and better. Our external circumstances are there to show us what we have decided internally are the conditions we are worthy of… they are simply signs of past and present choices we have made and are making. These can be changed!! If you are tolerating a life of less love, less acceptance, less joy decide today that you will make choices to change that less-than life.

> *Dear Lord, raise me up today! I know you have a plan for me that only includes abundance, love, and joy…I trust that the vision that you hold for my life is something that I am worthy in your image of moving into more fully. Help me. Reach down into my limited ways and views and lift me up in your ways, Lord. I petition you today for assistance to rise above the challenging circumstances, losses, and struggles in my life and place a new spirit of overcoming in me.*

> *Thank you, thank you, thank you for allowing me to live into this prayer today.*

DAY 16

Speak Your Truth

**"Trust in the Lord and do good;
dwell in the land and enjoy safe
pasture. Delight yourself in the
Lord and he will give you the
desires of your heart. Commit
your way to the Lord; trust in
him and he will do this; He will
make your righteousness shine
like the dawn, the justice of your
cause like the noonday sun."**

Psalm 36: 3-6

Every single one of us has a story. We all come with
a unique set of gifts, talents, skills, perspective, and
experiences. The world needs you to be the YOU-
iest you possible! Rising up today means owning that
vision of yourself operating in your place of strength.
Close your eyes and envision that place of strength
inside of you…where is it located in you? For many
people, when they stand up and close their eyes,

that place of strength and personal power is located squarely in their gut, in the solar plexus, in their core. Allow confidence and surety today to be located in your body. See yourself as your eyes are closed making choices from this place, having fun engaging conversations with others from this place...standing not in false confidence from a place of over-inflated ego but rather from the gentle KNOWING that you at your core are GOOD and WORTHY and can make choices and take actions from that place.

Ultimate humbleness requires that we admit that these unique capacities and life experiences were placed in us by God. We were gifted, blessed, and endowed with those things. Who are we to decide to keep that light under a bushel basket? He placed those in us for His uses and glory. He has a plan for you that comes from good, leads to good, and co-creates more good. Denying your own truth, your own story, cuts you off from acknowledging these gifts. Cuts you off from gratitude. Choose today to own your truth and your story for building His kingdom up. He wants your light to shine for all to see!

Dear Lord, you have created me uniquely to be your child holding all the special gifts, talents, skills, and experiences you have placed in me. Assist me today in confidently carrying forward this knowledge and apply them for

the good of the world you have so magnifi-
cently created. I trust that you have a plan and
a purpose for me, God....I trust that if I listen
and step out in willingness on what I hear, you
will lead me to glorify you through the use of
these gifts. Show me clearly how to do this
today so that I can magnify your goodness!

Thank you, thank you, thank you for allowing me to live into this prayer today.

DAY 17

Stronger and Stronger

**"Even youths grow tired and
weary, and young men stumble
and fall; but those who hope in
the Lord will renew their strength.
They will soar on wings like eagles;
they will run and not grow weary,
they will walk and not be faint."**

Isaiah 40: 30-31

Every day the Lord places in us a new capacity for
strength. Rising up in overcoming oftentimes means
we have to reach inside, turn to Him in pray, for new
levels of strength. Sometimes the magnitude of our
losses grieves our hearts in such a way that we simply don't know how to handle the depth of our hurt.
Lean into the Lord today and trust that He alone can
place the kind of strength in us that allows us to heal
and overcome those kinds of losses and hurts. We
don't have to know how we will feel stronger, we
don't have to figure anything out...we can simply

lean in and bring Him our weakness. He alone can turn it into strength and show us how to be grateful for the very circumstances that challenge us. The circumstances that challenge us are the very ones that the Lord is using to create remarkable capacity, resilience, and fortitude in us. You are being transformed into a mighty warrior with the strength of David inside of you.

Choose today to allow God to transform your human weakness into a superhuman strength. The depth of your compassion, your understanding, your empathy could not be what it is today without the very conditions in your life that you are working to overcome. Allow those to transform you today and choose to find your strength in God and give thanks for those challenges and circumstances! In doing that daily, you will become invincible, unbeatable… stronger and stronger!

Dearest Lord, thank you for giving me each and every day to grow in strength, wisdom, and courage. You have placed in me the spirit of a mighty warrior and today I pray that you reach inside me and work to ignite a fire in that warrior so that I may confidently go out into the world and do your work. I will rise above with your help! You amaze me with your grace, Lord. I am awestruck by the spirit of resiliency and perseverance you have placed in me. Help me recognize these as gifts you have graced me with and put them to good use today.

Thank you, thank you, thank you for allowing me to live into this prayer today.

DAY 18

Be the Instrument

"Have I not commanded you? Be strong and courageous. Do not be terrified; do not be discouraged, for the Lord your God will be with you wherever you go."

Joshua 1:9

When a new morning arrives it brings with it a new chance to begin again. Today you have an opportunity to rise up and be a vessel of Christ's love. You get to become the window that others can view true love through. We so often allow life and stopped up feelings and circumstances to cloud our vision from the highest and good that is available in every day situations. Today is your new opportunity to try a different way on for size and see how it feels. Get out of your own way today, set your own agenda aside and be truly present for God's will in each and every situation you are presented with today. If you are in the line at the grocery store and the person in front of you is complaining about the weather or their achy joints, take that moment to offer a smile or a kind word, help them turn their day around. Be the hands and feet of God today. Hold a door open, make a donation, pay a kindness forward, send a card of gratitude to a loved one.

The one thing we can always be sure of is that the plan for our life does not include our negativity or limited thinking to get in the way. If we truly want to embrace rising up in the spirit of overcoming and create a new reality in our lives, we must open up our eyes and heart to a different way of experiencing the moment-to-moment choices in our life. God wants you to be the vessel he pours His love onto others through. He placed us all here to be of service to one another. Today to choose to be the instrument only instead of trying to figure out what to write upon the canvas of your life. Let His love pour through you.

Dear God, today me be constantly reminded that it is not about me and the needs of my ego! Place in me your Spirit of unconditional love and compassion, the Spirit of willingness and courage to place myself in service to you, and the Spirit of stewardship so that I may be a shining example of you. Help me your hands and feet today, Lord. Remove my mind from the petty concerns of my everyday world and elevate my vision to the world's needs around me. Give me an elevated heart and mind so that I may remove my own limitations from the equation.

Thank you, thank you, thank you for allowing me to live into this prayer today.

DAY 19

How You Feel Matters

**"Peace I leave with you; my
peace I give to you. I do not give
to you as the world gives.   Do
not let your hearts be troubled
and do not be afraid."**

John 14:27

In our never-ceasing analytical world we very often
hear messages that logical thinking should reign over
emotion. That our feelings are somehow a substandard guide to decision-making or judgment and that
we must rely solely on thinking to solve problems. We
are complex creatures, designed to both think and feel.
Neither our thinking system nor our feeling system is
substandard. They work together to give us different
types of information. Today as you focus on co-creating
a new chapter in your life, recognize and acknowledge
your feelings as being a quality part of you. Your intuition and emotional center often times is a truer gauge
for spiritual information – God speaks to us through our
emotions to move us in directions with more compelling

action. If you tell yourself through thinking not to eat the chocolate cake because it is bad for you, but you overwhelmingly FEEL like eating the cake, you will more than likely eat the cake. Our emotions have the power to move us to action faster than our thinking.

Rising up to overcome challenges and setbacks often times encompasses honoring your feelings so that you can move through them. Denying that you are grieving or feel sad, angry, or frustrated and working to "push down" the emotion only serves to give it more power over you. Allow your feelings to be what they are – information. Allow them to rise up and be released so that you can move through them. They are a part of you but don't have to define you or your life.

Dear Lord, I recognize that you have perfectly placed all the parts of my being in me, my thoughts as well as my feelings. Help me today be reminded to be gentle with myself and honor my emotions. If there is pent up negative emotion in me, please, God, help me release those emotions so that they no longer have power over me. Only you know best the parts of me that need to be healed and opened up – I give myself over to you today, Lord, so that your healing can be done in me.

Thank you, thank you, thank you for allowing me to live into this prayer today.

DAY 20

Dance

"Shout for joy to the Lord, all the earth. Worship the Lord with gladness; come before him with joyful songs. Know that the Lord is God. It is he who made us, and we are his; we are his people, the sheep of his pasture. Enter his gates with thanksgiving and his courts with praise; give thanks to him and praise his name. For the Lord is good and his love endures forever; his faithfulness continues through all generations."

PSALM 100

Yesterday you allowed emotions to be a quality part of you...today allow joy in and celebrate movement through dance! Dancing with the universe doesn't have to mean literally dancing with your feet...for you it might mean listening to a favorite song really loud in the car while you are driving with the windows rolled down. It might mean taking a walk down the street in the rain, allowing the feel of the raindrops to wash over you and make you feel like splashing in the puddles. There are all kinds of ways we experience joy but the main thing to align yourself with today is the action of getting into joyful movement. Creating a new reality means plugging in with a new mentality and emotionality....and that can happen much more effortlessly with a new physicality. Sitting on the couch will not get the job done! Sitting hunched over a computer will not do it! You must stretch your legs and arms and increase your heart rate with happiness a little.

Each and every day is a victory over death! You are alive, you are vibrant, you are here! Celebrate that simple fact by embracing the dance of life and engaging with the universe today. Shrug off feelings of sadness, guilt, depression, overwhelm, confusion and simply choose to push the pause button on those today. You DO have a choice! God placed in us a joyful, fun spirit...music speaks to this spirit for many of us. Dance with the Lord today and let yourself feel joy. Your day will be amazing if you do!

Dear God, today I give myself over to your joy and your celebration of life through me! Place in me a happy, light spirit of being so that can let go and allow my joy to come forward. I love you, Lord! If I run away from you, you find me...if I run towards you, you welcome me...you are truly amazing! Place me music in my heart and in my life today so that I can praise and worship, raising my energy and the very life force you originally designed in me. Let me throw open the gateways, set aside my worries and anxieties, and dance today in spite of them, in gratitude of the blessings you have placed all around me!

Thank you, thank you, thank you for allowing me to live into this prayer today.

DAY 21

Move into the Light

**"Come to me, all you who are
weary and burdened, and I will give
you rest. Take my yoke upon you
and learn from me, for I am gentle
and humble in heart, and you will
rest for your souls. For my yoke
is easy and my burden is light."**

MATTHEW 11: 28-30

Bless you for dancing yesterday! Today you get to continue this joyful momentum and expand into your new reality to an even greater degree. Moving into the light means choosing to only see the possibilities today. Rising up and overcoming challenges means seeing the circumstances of our lives from a different perspective. Put on your God-colored glasses today. How could your environment be changed to reflect the new forward-feeling you are working to create in your life? Could you move something away from the window and literally let in more light? Could you throw away clutter that is bogging down your spirit? Could you paint a room yellow or orange or another bright cheery color that freshens and brightens up everything? "What if…?" is the motto of the day today! What if I…….? Finish the sentence with your own new possibility.

What if you took a walk through your life as an observer today and asked this question about every aspect of it. What if you embraced a new level of health today? What would that look like? What new information, people, places could that involve? Would there be things you would need to clear out of the house, out of the pantry, out of your brain? Is there old, dark self-talk holding you back from living into better health today? What if you opened yourself to new relationships today? What would that look like? Would that mean moving out of your routine some and embracing a new group, activity, or environment? What if you adopted a new commitment to your finances today? What different actions would you need to take to feel lighter and more proactive today in that area? Asking ourselves open-ended questions allows us to move into a more expansive, lighter space of possibility, hope, and a new future reality. Use your imagination and fling open every door and window! God is waiting for you to invite in His light!

Dear Lord, I know if I rely on my power alone I cut off so much of what is available to me. Through you and in you, so much more creative energy is available. Breathe a quietness of mind into me today such that I can be available in a new way to listen to what you are calling me to do. Show me how to get off the treadmill of busyness and anxiety, stilling my heart and centering my mind on you and your will for my life. I trust that if I open up to you in a new way you will guide me patiently to a new day, Lord.

Thank you, thank you, thank you for allowing me to live into this prayer today.

DAY 22

Co-create Your Tomorrows

"Consider it your joy, my brothers, whenever you face trials of many kinds, because you know that the testing of your faith develops perseverance. Perseverance must finish its work so that you may be mature and complete, not lacking in anything."

James 1: 2-4

When listening to people tell their stories very often what we hear is that "this happened or that happened" to them as if they had no part in bringing that experience into their life. Part of the great responsibility for free will that God placed in our life is owning and be accountable for our part in co-creating our lives through our minute-to-minute choices. Every time we choose what to eat, we are choosing what we are fueling our body with to rebuild cells with. We are consciously or subconsciously making co-creative choices every single hour, every day. It is staggering actually how many choices we make every day. Thousands of seemingly minute decisions that shape our lives in a very powerful way. We choose our health, we choose our relationships, we choose our finances. In order to rise up and overcome challenges is owning our role and responsibility to making these choices.

Choose today to take an extremely proactive role in actively, consciously CHOOSING what brings you joy, what builds you and others up, what you LOVE in your life. Just as it takes a large cruise ship a good amount of distance to turn around, expect that new results from your new choices may not show up overnight. Be patient and diligent in your application of your powers of choice. God placed an amazing resilient spirit in you because He knows you are extremely powerful in your ability to co-create a new tomorrow in your life. Own this spirit of overcoming…own your power as a co-creator with the Lord and make good, empowering choices!

What a wonderful God you are! Thank you for allowing me to participate in creating choices for my life. Help me take full responsibility for this awesome responsibility and ability. Lord, as I move into closer relationship with you allow me to make right choices that only serve to draw me closer to you and your great love. Help me see that every choice I make either moves me closer or further apart. I want to be in step with you and co-create with you, Lord. As you work to move me into a better restored life, help me see each and every choice as an opportunity to be in sync with you!

Thank you, thank you, thank you for allowing me to live into this prayer today.

DAY 23
Listen

**"The righteous cry out, and the
Lord hears them; he delivers them
from all their troubles. The Lord
is close to the brokenhearted
and saves those who are crushed
in spirit. A righteous man may
have many troubles, but the Lord
delivers him from them all."**

Psalm 34: 17-19

We are surrounded by the noise of the world. TV, radio, media of all kinds, others' voices...the noise of the world just simply is almost impossible to get away from unless we make a conscious choice to quiet our environment. Today rising above means rising above the noise and quieting our minds and hearts. For the past several days you have been busy shaking things up – moving, dancing, changing your environment, your conditions and mindsets. Today is about stillness. About finding that small space inside that craves silence, craves a retreat into a safe, warm, womblike place. It is a homecoming of sorts because that place always exists in us if we choose to acknowledge it.

In this space of stillness, ask God for guidance, tell Him the concerns of your heart. Even tell Him if you feel you don't know how to pray or how to hear His voice. God speaks to us regularly when we are listening but it comes in many forms. Sometimes it is still, small God-whispers, a reference to a person, place, or thing we are needing to connect with. Sometimes all we hear is the silence and it is almost deafening. In those moments God offers us an opportunity to wait, to be practice patience in learning His timing, His will unfolding at His pace. Sometimes we listen and we hear "Wait. Be still. Do not fear. I am here." It can be frustrating not to get immediate answers but He is faithful and never ignores our prayers. Practice stilling yourself, asking, and listening today. Turn off the noise of the world and connect with a deeper place. Your spirit thirsts for rest and peace in this way...honor its need for quiet.

> *Dear Lord, I am listening today as you have instructed me to. More than that I am asking you to show me not only a path to recovery, a path out of grieving my losses and past hurts, but also to show me your path to purpose*

for my life. What is the next natural step you would like me to take? Are you calling me to have the courage to take that next step? Lord, if so, please give me all the strength and wisdom to discern your voice speaking to me. Do not send just gentle nudges but speak into my life with full authority your plans for me. I place myself lovingly at your feet today, Lord.

Thank you, thank you, thank you for allowing me to live into this prayer today.

DAY 24

Trust

**"But blessed is the man who trusts
in the Lord, whose confidence
is in him. He will be like a tree
planted by the water and sends
out its roots by the stream. It
does not fear when heat comes;
its leaves are always green. It has
no worries in a year of drought
and never fails to bear fruit."**

JEREMIAH **17: 7-8**

When we have been hurt or experienced a loss, trusting again is one of the hardest parts of recovery for
many. Trusting others, trusting ourselves, even trusting God is challenged as we lick our wounds, asking
ourselves sometimes over and over again "Why?"
Oftentimes, there are not direct answers to this
question...we are not given insight into our losses
and setbacks in the moment. Sometimes we are not
even given that insight in hindsight many years later.

Trusting that everything we are entrusted with, including our painful experiences and challenges and losses, was given to us with a purpose that can be turned to good is something we need to work on as we choose to rise and overcome. As overcomers, we have already chosen that our setbacks in our health, our relationships, or our finances will not define us. Our pasts will not define our futures. We speed up this process of moving forward as we speed up the process of learning to trust again. Opening ourselves up to risks – being vulnerable to more pain through loving wide open, trying again, taking chances – even the risk of holding hope in our hearts for we might be disappointed yet once again – is not always easy. Be gentle with yourself today as you meditate on trust. Know that God is with you as you relearn trust.

As children, we naturally trust and try, trust and try, again and again. We don't have enough experiences under our belts yet to put up defenses and be cynical, skeptical, afraid. Practice being childlike in your trusting today…open yourself to new places, people, resources, and opportunities by removing your defenses. Let your guard down and invite in courage and trust. All of this and more is being worked for your good!!

Dear Lord, I have been lost and have been challenged in ways only you know. You alone know all the worries and anxieties of my heart. You alone know my loneliness at times, feeling like I was carrying the weight of the world on my shoulders. I trust you have been working all the circumstances and trials in my life for good and on my behalf. I trust that you will lead me and guide me with your loving ways. Today especially, I fully extend every ounce of trust I have in my body, my mind, my heart, and my spirit, knowing that even this very moment is perfect in its design.

Thank you, thank you, thank you for allowing me to live into this prayer today.

DAY 25

The Next Natural Step

**"I have set the Lord always before
me. Because he is at my right
hand, I will not be shaken."**

Psalm **16:8**

What do we do next? Rising above our circumstances
takes action. There is no doubt about it. If we don't
do anything different than we are doing today we are
sure to get more of what we have already gotten. It
is time to move forward. It is time to move on. Today
is all about inspired action. Inspired action is different than other types of action. It is not an unnatural,
grasping-at-straws desperate type of action or a ran-
dom, let-me-take-a-stab-at-it kind of action. It is the
kind of action that is inspired by love, by God. Where
does our interest, joy, love naturally lead us? What
are we naturally inspired to investigate, do, or want
to have? What are we attracted to organically? This
is again where our emotions come into play over our
thinking and logical brain centers. Allowing ourselves

to naturally be led by what doesn't feel forced is an art and it creates inspired action. Maybe you have had a recurring idea or thought...why are you waiting to action on it? Jump! Let go of having to know where it leads or what it means...it will be revealed to you! Allow yourself to be moved into action.

Taking the next natural step requires courage. Sometimes that next step is a big one...sometimes it is simply a baby step. Consider that God's plan is unfolding naturally for you and through you by allowing yourself to step out in courage and inspiration. We are taught and conditioned in school to only use our thinking and logic to guide our actions but taking part in this kind of action requires a heart-centered, intuition-grounded approach to decision making. Picture your life as a giant flow chart – one choice leads you one direction and another leads you on a completely different path. Sometimes we are getting internal guidance from our GPS (God Positioning System) and we are afraid to take the step laid in front of us. Act in spite of fear and do it anyways. Let God be the navigator in your life! His divine wisdom is so much greater than our own and He has plans for you that are so much greater than you can imagine!

Dear Lord, sometimes I do not know the way to go! You give me choices and I know I have free will but so many times I feel either confused or backed into choices due to circumstance. Help me stand strong in you, Lord. Help me understand how infinite your love is for me and that you will unfailingly guide me if I submit myself to you. I love you, Lord! I choose you! I choose new life in you!

Thank you, thank you, thank you for allowing me to live into this prayer today.

DAY 26

Celebrate

**"Therefore I tell you, do not worry
about your life, what you will
eat or drink; or about your body,
what you will wear. Is not life
more important than food, and
the body more important than
clothes? Look at the birds of the
air; they do not sow or reap or
store away in barns, and yet your
heavenly Father feeds them. Are
you not much more valuable than
they? Who of you by worrying
can add a single hour to his life?"**

***Matthew* 6: 25-27**

You did it! You took the next natural step and tried
inspired action on for size...how did it feel? Did you
feel uncomfortable and like you were treading on unknown ground? That is a good sign! Remember if
you take different actions you are guaranteed different results. Congratulations on your courage!

Today is a day of celebration. You are celebrating freedom today as you ARE overcoming and rising above those challenges and obstacles that have gotten in your way. You are celebrating your ability to choose something better. You are celebrating the gifts, experiences, talents, skills, and perspectives the Lord has placed in your life! Were you born into generations of poverty mentality, poor health choices, or unhealthy relationship and communication patterns? Yes, celebrate even those! Those are the things that were placed in your life to give you opportunities for experiential learning and strength. Would you be the person you are without those external circumstances? No! Give thanks and celebrate everything good and bad you have been given. Every person, situation, and lesson. Give thanks for your loved ones and your enemies. Give thanks for the injustice and even the violence in our world as it instructs you on what you choose instead. Without bad, good wouldn't be recognized or appreciated. It is only after the darkness, we can appreciate the day break! God has placed a new day and a new spirit in you to overcome and not simply survive, but THRIVE and celebrate your life in the light of this new day!

Thank you, God! Thank you for renewing hope in my spirit, for placing a joyful heart in me! Thank you for giving me courage to face each new day and recognize not only the

opportunities its offers but the reciprocal responsibility you have placed in me to choose
life over death each and every day! Breathe
into me today, Lord, the continued Spirit of
new life, of recovery from losses of the past
and the ability to step forward with a new
perspective, new energy, and new joy!

Thank you, thank you, thank you for allowing me to live into this prayer today.

DAY 27

Two Steps Forward, One Step Back

**"Do not let your hearts be
troubled. Trust in God."**

JOHN 14:1

Patience. Patience, my child. Although we many time
wish that moving forward happened in one fell swoop
or in a perfect linear path, most times it does not. It is
akin to building muscle strength – one day we show
up at the gym and have a strong day of progress,
making several strides forward and feeling encour-
aged and proud of ourselves, only to show up the
very next day feeling overwhelmed, underpowered,
and weaker than ever. Rising up while overcoming
challenges in our health, relationships, or finances
can operate exactly like this. We will have several
strong days and then find ourselves regressing a bit.
Think of the ocean waves – only in their periodic re-
ceding do they regain power to charge forward again
with even more gusto and force.

We are part of God's natural plan. We have
seasons in our energy and our inspiration, much

the same way there are seasons in nature. Part of overcoming is honoring those seasons in grieving our losses and setbacks and charging forward in reshaping our lives with trust and courage on the strong days. Be gentle and kind to yourself as you recognize and experience both the yin and the yang of life. God has placed both complementary energies together for good in you. Healing and regaining trust and confidence in yourself and the world is not a straightforward process. Even children when they are growing into the next stage, moving out of their cribs for example, have a night now and then when they just want to crawl back inside the safety of that old place, that old way. We don't always need to succumb to it, but it is good to recognize that it is natural and expected so you can be aware and easy on yourself along the journey.

Dear Lord, each and every day you teach me patience. Thank you for the opportunity to recognize the wisdom in your timing and that there will be days when I don't feel as strong. I trust that especially in these days you will teach me how to be renewed in my faith, to learn an even deeper level of trust, and to learn how to look even closer for your blessings in each and every day. Help me learn how to breathe deeply on these days, steady-ing myself in my knowing of your steadfast love and blessing over my life.

Thank you, thank you, thank you for al-lowing me to live into this prayer today.

DAY 28

The Gratitude Bridge

**"Give thanks to the Lord, for
He is good; His love endures
forever. Give thanks to the God
of gods. His love endures forever.
Give thanks to the Lord of lords:
His love endures forever."**

PSALM 136:1-3

As we give thanks daily three times in succession, to
the Father, the Son, and the Holy Spirit, invite new
ideas, new inspiration, and new blessings. Gratitude
is the bridge to even more abundance – there is no
other bridge that we can cross to get us there. We
cannot fake or manufacture our gratitude...it must
come from a real and authentic place in our hearts.
We can either look around us and see all that there is
to be grateful for, no matter what our circumstances,
or we cannot. Sometimes we can see what we should
feel grateful for but we don't actually FEEL the gratitude. Taking time to name those things, to focus on

what about them brings goodness into your life, why those people, places, things or opportunities bless your life will help you tap into the feeling of gratitude. Working words of gratitude, joy, and love into your language regularly will also help you feel those things more regularly.

Today, as we continue to strengthen ourselves in our commitment to rise above and overcome, allowing the Holy Spirit to fill us with recognition of all that is good and blessed in our lives, we focus on inviting in gratitude. Step out today and tell the people around you what you are grateful for – no strings attached, looking for nothing in return – just speak it out loud. Thank your family, your neighbors, your pastor or priest, your boss, your coworkers – look and see all there is to be grateful for and overwhelm them with your overt spirit of enthusiasm and thankfulness. Smile and look people in the eye as you express this – they will be astonished by the love light and the twinkle in your eye!

Dearest Lord, I am growing in my awareness of how each and every circumstance was planted in my life for a purpose. Each and every person. Each and every resource and opportunity. How great are your blessings! Hold me closer in gratitude each day so that this awareness just becomes a natural extension of my thinking and being, so that I can walk fully with you, Lord. I am so very grateful for my life, for the very breath in my body...thank you! I look around me and everywhere I look I see a reminder of your great love for us!

Thank you, thank you, thank you for allowing me to live into this prayer today.

DAY 29

Miracles All Around Us

**"You're blessed when you get
your inside world – your mind and
heart – put right. Then you can
see God in the outside world"**

*MATTHEW **5:8***

Every direction we turn, every place that we look we
will see and hear of miracles. Is it possible that miracles are in fact not the exception but God's norm?
If we invite people to share their stories, we will hear
about seemingly chance encounters and reunions,
surprising blessings, amazing events of healing and
restoration. It seems that what we seek, we find.
What we ask for, we do in fact, receive. God is amazing in His abundance!

Is it then possible that the only reason we have
been feeling stuck in our recovery is that we have not
been seeing, really seeing, what is right in front of us
the whole time? Is it at all possible that everything
we really need is right in front of us and has been for

some time? In my own life, for the longest time as I was praying for answers and guidance on the next step in my recovery, what I now recognize is that the miraculous answers to my prayers were quite often in front of me the whole time! God had placed all the resources I needed to restore my health squarely in my path and I had chosen to defend against them and ignore them! God had placed all the skills and capacities in me that I needed for a financial recovery in my life and I chose to contract and feel defeated and confused rather than step out in confidence and gratitude, embracing the amazing gifts He had placed in me! God had placed the love of my life right on my doorstep and I chose to retreat from him in shame before opening my eyes to the blessing that he truly was to me! Yikes!! It is staggering to me how all these miracles had occurred all around me, right in front of my own eyes, and I had chosen not to see them as such. What glaringly obvious blessings are you blocking yourself in receiving? Rise up, overcome, and get out of your own way already!

The mystery of you, Lord, is evident all around me! You answer our prayers for healing and intercession, you work all things behind the scenes for our good…thank you, Lord! Today help me see all your miracles and recognize that they are all around me, happening without me having to do anything to deserve them or make them happen. You have looked into my life and brought me perfectly to this prayer today, this moment of recognition of your greatness. Allow me to accept these miracles as my new normal and feel your presence in my life all the time as I step forward into this new life.

Thank you, thank you, thank you for allowing me to live into this prayer today.

DAY 30

Commitment

**"God is our refuge and strength,
an ever-present help in trouble.
Therefore we will not fear,
though the earth give way and
mountains fall into the heart of
the sea, though its waters roar
and foam and mountains quake
and with their surging."**

PSALM 46: 1-3

Rise up and overcome. Christ rose up over death and already completed the covenant He had with us. All of our weaknesses have been covered by His strength. Love for Him above all else can put the wind beneath our wings that we need to move forward with Him first and foremost.

If you have not made the commitment to put the Lord first in your life, in your relationships, in your household and your finances, commit to do that today. The vow He made to us to love us unconditionally does not waver according to conditions or circumstances. Neither should our love and commitment waver according to conditions or circumstances. Even as I write this, I received an email outlining the journey of a wife praying for renewed commitment and reconciliation in her broken marriage, even after divorce, as she contemplated the loving marriage and commitment she had made to God so many years before. Her fervent prayers were answered as she recognized her commitment to forgiving and loving the way that Jesus forgives and loves us. Miracles all around us! Today is a new day, a new beginning, a new journey...rise up as a strong warrior and fight through sadness, grieving, anger, vengeance, and guilt as you recommit your life to God. You can rise from the ashes, stronger than ever!

Dearest Lord, I am committed to you! I ask you to place a new spirit of love and joy in me so that I may have all the energy and life in me that you designed for me from my very moment of birth. I rise up in you today, Lord, and commit to being yours over and over again, all the days of my life, forever remembering that you in turn pledged your whole life to me in turn. Thank you, God, for this amazing new day, this amazing new way in my life!

Thank you, thank you, thank you for allowing me to live into this prayer today.

Future

VIII.

Envisioning a Better Way... *or a Better Day*

"Our greatest glory is not in never falling,
but in rising every time we fall."

— *CONFUCIUS*

We create in our lives what we can visualize with our thoughts. We won't climb a mountain unless we can envision ourselves climbing. We won't buy a house unless we can envision ourselves living there. We create our "comfort zones" not only from our previous experiences but in the limitations we place on our own visualization. You hear all the time about how "if you can see it, you can achieve it." We hear about professional athletes spending time before every game, every putt, every throw, envisioning the end result that they desire and their body responds. They are able to create what they saw in their mind's eye. The power of their thoughts becomes, in fact, their personal capacity for action and creating their desired outcomes.

Likewise, in order to rebound from any personal set-back or failure, you must envision, you must think about what your life looks like having already rebounded. Is it a new career you desire? Put yourself in the shoes of some-one already having that career. What would that person do when they woke up every day, what would they wear? What would their daily activities look like? Envision yourself put-ting on those clothes, performing those activities. Can you *see* it? Now what would it *feel* like to be in that new career? Would you feel proud of yourself for having rebounded and moved on, creating a new direction for yourself? Would you call someone to tell them about your accomplishment? Create as much vivid detail as possible until you actually create the good feelings associated with already having achieved it. Allow yourself to feel those happy feelings, that glow that comes from having accomplished something that you desired, having attained a place beyond where you are in your grieving today.

It is absolutely critical that you are able to do this. A lot of times, we are still so confused about how to unravel the mess that we are in, we can't decide what we want. We don't know our future, we are still in the aftermath and that has created a void, a lack of direction, clarity, or confidence. That void will be filled one day with something positive again, I know. Today it may feel like that hole will always be there, and there probably will always be some pain when you look back, but it won't be the hard, throbbing ache of loss that it is now.

If you are in that space, don't pressure yourself to figure it all out. Trust that it will come. Instead, envision yourself feeling better. You don't have to know why you feel better, you just do. Envision yourself in a favorite place, laughing at something a loved one said or did, feeling content and peaceful inside about the future. Feeling secure and safe in that moment to unwind and let loose, have fun. Stretch your arms out while you are envisioning this. It is almost impossible to feel sad, hurt, alone, confused, angry, or depressed when you have your arms outstretched. In fact, don't be surprised if while you are doing this visualization, you want to smile. In this way, our actions oftentimes <u>precede</u> our feelings.

Waiting until you feel better to take positive actions is like waiting for the cart to lead the horse. Did you ever push past the feeling of not wanting to do something and just did it, only to find yourself actually enjoying doing it after all? Although I now consider myself a regular exerciser, there is rarely a day that I feel like working out. I like the feeling I have afterwards, but I really don't relish the thought of working out and typically I don't feel completely positive about it. It is still easier, after years of doing it, for me to avoid it or find a reason I really don't have time or can't exercise. However, when I push past the feeling of not wanting to do it, after about 10 minutes I start feeling positive about exercising. It happens time and time again, so now I know that I must take the action BEFORE I feel like doing it if I desire the outcome. This is so counterintuitive that I consider it one of the most important things to learn from this book. If you don't take anything else away, take away this: Action leads to

Feeling. And what proceeds action? You got it...Visualization. If I couldn't visualize myself exercising, feeling great afterwards and enjoying the outcome, I would be a lot less likely to begin taking any action in that direction. You get the picture!

To rebound, you must envision yourself having already rebounded. Take action on that vision, and then, and only then, will you feel better. Are you seeing a cycle here? We have explored this positive cycle and where it leads because it is such a critical path of understanding. We also looked at the flip side, the down cycle so that you can see where that leads. Since we have examined both of these, perhaps now you will see how imperative your act of making a choice in your own process actually is. I'm not saying "well, just snap out of it," I'm trying to show you HOW to do that. How to choose to rebound rather than live in the past and present hurt and future anxiety and fear.

Rebounding Top Ten List

Note to self: Remember that getting there is all the fun!

1. Learn as you go and be curious about the next step.
2. Be understanding of the process.
3. Be patient enough to let time be your ally, not your enemy.

4. Write your epitaph in an affectionate manner:
    What did you do while here on earth? What was your legacy?

5. Write a six-month "Personal Promise" want list.
    Your "Personal Promise" list is a list of goals.
    Not a list of simple items "it would be nice" to do, be, or have...
    this is a list of the things you PROMISE yourself to do, be, or have.

6. Write a paragraph about each want on your "Personal Promise" list.
    Tape this list somewhere.

7. Check your list and ask yourself two "Personal Promise" questions:
    Is your personal <u>why</u> for wanting this strong enough to carry you past inevitable obstacles and speed-bumps?
    What is the next natural step toward fulfilling your personal promises?

8. Be sure you stay physically active and practice good self-care.

9. Spend 5-10 minutes a day in private meditation, prayer, or visualization. Envision yourself fulfilling your personal promises - how do you look, feel, and sound in your vision?

10. Complete the 21-day Rebounding Radical Action Plan (can be downloaded at *theresabassett.com*)

Failure should be our teacher, not our undertaker.
Failure is delay, not defeat. It is a tempo-
rary detour, not a dead-end street.

What has your setback taught you or what
is it trying to teach you right now?
What opportunities for growth is God offering you?

IX.

Rising Up to Overcome

"When I am weak, then I am strong."

– 2 COR. 12:10

First and foremost, this book and the inquiry that leads from it have been inspired by God and planted in me, to come through me, and to be used as a tool for healing. My intentions and prayers around this work are to provide individuals and organizations with a needed breath of renewal and grace. Ideally, one would find hope and solace and perhaps a path of self-discovery and self-forgiveness here that would lead to inspired action and fuel for their new chapters ahead. We have all been gifted such remarkable opportunities for renewal, right down to a cellular level. Continuous renewal is an important part of total wellness and sustainability. Total wellness of the individual is in fact the building block of the total wellness of our greater societal framework. Without this we are nothing. God has planted in us, through His grace and infinite love, everything we need. By turning to Him in prayer, we unlock a treasure chest of vast resources.

He planted in us an engine of renewal and growth that we are anointed to be good stewards of. By recognizing the truth available in God's grace, we are allowed not just renewal but *TRANSFORMATION*. If we choose not to care for or feed this engine we see contraction, disintegration, and a true withering of spirit. I have ultimate faith in humanity. I have faith in the system that God placed in the universe to govern our growth. Just as the Universe spirals outward and is mirrored in every sea shell, we are designed internally as tiny mirrors of the greater whole. The earth is regenerative just as we are regenerative. Being responsible stewards of this system requires us to pay attention and learn what we can about taking good care - slowing down long enough to understand. It is sometimes in our greatest setbacks, that we finally slow down, or stop, to pay attention. It allows a chance to become deeply aware or our own humanity, vulnerability, and of God's true blessings.

I have watched my marriage, my finances, and my health disintegrate. I have watched them regenerate as well. We are brought to "rock bottom" at times because there, and only there, can we find the emotional energy to move ourselves into an expansive, action-oriented state. While we are grieving our losses, our selves, our spirits, and our bodies are in the process of becoming more rigid, of contracting and in this state one choice only leads to another disempowering choice. But then something remarkable happens.

We either expand or die. Atrophy is only an option for so long. There are built-in checks and balances. For our bodies, our relationships, as well as our finances. We can look at a myriad of physical, financial, relational, or political problems but at their core they are really very simple. Somewhere along the line, these systems ceased to be fed quality fuel. The nutrients dried up or the love dried up or the money dried up or the work dried up or our energy to problem-solve dried up. And at that point we simply stopped expanding into the next empowering choice and started merely surviving., getting through the next day of pain or the next school day full of chaos or the next work week full of monotony or the next year full of loss.

Love has the power to reverse all of that. And God grants us endless supplies of it by breathing into us His Holy Spirit. And that binds us all together.

No matter what our culture, our geography, our religion, or training, our education, our belief systems...we all have certain things in common and these transcend all boundaries: The need to be loved. The need to create. The need to be deeply nourished and fed. The need to feel significant.

And no result comes about without an action. Action…. Reaction. Action….Consequence. Action…Result.

This book is about creating inspired action that leads to inspired results: actions of love, actions of stewardship. As we take deeply loving and nourishing actions from this place of acknowledging a need for renewal and rebirth, we are given a chance to spiral outward, taking actions that result in contributing to the growth and progress of the world around us. However, we must first put on our own oxygen masks before reaching across the aisle and helping another. Breathe in love, breathe out love. Breathe in spirit, breathe out spirit. Breathe in God's grace, breathe out God's grace.

We *can* rebuild our bodies. We *can* rebuild our relationships. We *can* rebuild our finances. We *can* rebuild our LIVES. Rising up to overcome creates a rebounding revolution of love that spirals downward into our core selves and spirals outward as an ever-flowing expression of God's unconditional love through us.

Rebounding isn't a static process. It isn't just a 30-day process and it really can't be reduced to some written bits of self-help advice, but you have to start somewhere and sometimes a springboard is just what the doctor ordered. It is a completely dynamic, personal, intimate, *active* process by which you become conscious of who you really are, what you are truly made of, and where you truly want to go. It is a process of becoming aware of the whole range of choices available to you whether you like them or not, and choosing…and then choosing again, and then again, maybe course correcting and choosing something different…It is raw, it makes us vulnerable to risk and reward, success and failure, our self-concept, our story, our self-esteem, our patterns of self-care, and to the up and down cycles of life.

Suffice it to say that there are many shadows around many an unseen corner. The sunshine moments in our lives will be made better, will become the stuff that gratitude is made of by the simple recognition of these shadows and for these too, we give thanks. According to Nancy Anderson in her book, *Work with Passion*, "You know you have arrived when you see all of your experiences as necessary to your growth. As you look back at past choices, you understand that you did the best you could at the time, given your level of awareness. You are patient with yourself during this process, forgiving yourself quickly for not seeing what may now seem obvious. You know that awakening from emotional numbness takes time, so you do not rush that dynamic process. As soon as a shift in your thinking occurs, insight comes."

This is the stage of the rebounding process in which you have admitted to yourself that in all your imperfection, you are undeniably *right here* and you want to continue embracing God's grace, moving forward in the most positive way possible. For me, today, part of this is about coming into the space where I could share this with you, see my own truth, and hope that you would share it with others that may be working through their own rebounding process. Rise up to overcome, fellow Rebounders!

Thank you, thank you, thank you.

About the Author

Originally from Royal Oak, Michigan, Theresa Bassett is an international speaker and the author of a Christian non-fiction book entitled, ***Rebounding: A Practical Guide for Getting Up (and Getting Over It!)*** (AuthorHouse 2010) and co-author of the book entitled, ***YES You Can! Reaching Your Potential While Achieving Greatness*** (Insight Publishing, 2011). She is also the co-founder of Bailey's Books, a non-profit dedicated to distributing inspirational books worldwide and the CEO of Heart+Hammer (Heart-Hammer.com), a strategic market-ing and advertising agency. As an inspired entrepreneur since

2006, Theresa is a master leadership coach and trainer. She previously owned a boutique coaching agency named Inspire, Inc. and while there was Covey certified to teach the *7 Habits of Highly Effective People* and the *8th Habit*. She is also a certified Tony Robbins coach, Masterstream sales coach and trainer, and is a licensed real estate professional with over $250M in personal sales.

Theresa is a graduate of Michigan State University, attended graduate school at North Carolina State University and previously published the book ***Yes, You Can (2013)***. She currently lives in Raleigh, NC with husband Kelley Bassett. They have three children: Shelby (age 22), Katrina (age 18), and Arben (age 16). They enjoy frequent trips to coastal areas, time with family, and long walks with their dog, Bella.

You can learn more about Theresa at theresabassett.com or email her team directly at info@theresabassett.com for specific inquiries regarding her availability for coaching or speaking engagements. You can also register to attend her latest Rebounding Revolution webinar at theresabassett.com/webinar.

Share Your Story

If you'd like to share your story with me privately or you'd like to share it publically, there are options for doing that. I'd love to hear your story so that I can pray for your recovery and your journey specifically. Visit *theresabassett.com* and Click the "Share Your Story" button. You can also visit the *Rebounding Revolution* Facebook page and share your story with others so that a wider community may pray with you and offer support.

Select Bibliography

The Bible, New International Version. Thomas Nelson Press, 2013.

Barry, Douglas. Wisdom for a Young CEO: Incredible Letters and Inspiring Advice from Today's Business Leaders. Philadelphia, London: Running Press, 2004.

Booher, Diana. Get a Life Without Sacrificing Your Career: How to Make More Time for What's Really Important. New York, San Francisco, et al.: Mc-Graw-Hill, 1997.

Canfield, Jack, and Mark Victor Hansen. Chicken Soup for the Soul: 101 Stories to Open the Heart & Rekindle the Spirit. Deerfield Beach, Florida: Health Communications, 1993.

Carlson, Richard, and Benjamin Shield. Handbook for the Soul. Boston, New York, et al.: Little, Brown, and Co., 1995.

Chandler, Steve. The Story of You: (And How to Create a New One). Franklin Lakes, NJ: Career Press, 2006.

Kotter, PhD., Jeffrey. Private Moments. Secret Selves: Enriching our Time Alone. New York: Ballantine Books, 1990.

Motwane, Aman. <u>Yes, You Can Change the World</u>. Redono Beach, California: Prakash Press, 2007.

Ruiz, Don Miguel. <u>The Four Agreements</u>. San Rafael, California: Amber-Allen, 1997.

Tracy, Brian. <u>The Psychology of Achievement</u>. Niles, Illinois: Nightingale Conant, 1987.

Wooden, Coach John, and Steve Jamison. <u>Wooden: A Lifetime of Observations and Reflections On and Off the Court</u>. New York: McGraw-Hill, 1997.

Ward, Bernard. <u>Think Yourself Well. The Amazing Power of Your Mind</u>. New York: Globe Communications, 1994.

Special Opportunities and Offers

There are a number of ways we can support one another and help each other grow. Setbacks come in all sizes and shapes – personal and professional – and it is important not only to share your story with others but share other resources as well. Recovery can only happen once we are able to own the gifts God planted in our journey and have the willingness to offer those gifts to others as well.

Visit TheresaBassett.com to order a FREE downloadable Rebounding Journal so that you can begin to capture the specific gifts planted in your journey. Look for the FREE GIFT section or go directly to theresabassett.com/journal for your copy.

Also, we have created a non-profit called Bailey's Books in order to collect and distribute motivational and inspirational books to others who may need a lift along their path. Visit BaileysBooks.org to learn how to contribute. We know God oftentimes works through words to inspire and lift us, plant seeds of hope, and speak "next steps" into our lives. Please consider giving back by sending us books, contributing monetarily to the inspirational literacy movement we are creating, or founding a distribution site. A full list of current distribution sites is also available online.

To contact Theresa directly please email her at Theresa@theresabassett.com.

Small Group/Book Club Resources

A discussion and study guide will be available for book club, small group, women's or church group purposes. For more information or volume order information, please email info@ theresabassett.com.

Other Bassett Group Companies:

Heart+Hammer is a full service strategic marketing and advertising agency with headquarters in Raleigh, NC. The focus of this company is to help businesses create sales and marketing traction with their brand. Visit Heart-Hammer. com for more information or to schedule a free marketing consultation.

Made in the USA
Columbia, SC
05 May 2017